Looking After...

Beverly Leach
aka
Ruth Ghio

Copyright ©2026 by Beverly Leach aka Ruth Ghio

Arena Press
Grass Valley, CA

Original cover and book design: Adden Design

Cover photo: author's private collection

All rights reserved. This book or any portion thereof may not be reproduced or used in any manner without the express written permission of the author, except for the use of brief quotations in a book review, or as permitted by U.S. copyright law.

ISBN: 979-8-9893956-2-0

Dedicated to my parents
Edna and Ralph Leach
and
Ruth Lambert, my grandmother.
Without these people there would be no story.

I also dedicate this book
to my Finnish relatives and ancestors
who played a larger role
in my development than I imagined.

I also wrote this book for my four children:
Charlotte, Beth, Tony, and Kathy
who were also affected by this story
and may have never known
what in the hell was happening.

Looking After...

Beverly Leach
aka
Ruth Ghio

Beverly Joyce
Elvin Ralph   Charles Franklin
Irwin Roy

Leach Family

Charles Franklin	Irwin Roy	Elvin Ralph
Beverly Joyce	Edgar Ralph (father)	Edna Muriel (mother)

Contents

The Couple 13

Introduction 19

Chapter 1
   Marriage and the Birth of Charlotte 21

Chapter 2
   Oakland: Adjusting to Marriage 27

Chapter 3
   Red Bluff: Beth's Birth in Oakland 33

Chapter 4
   Settling into Red Bluff: Work and Family 39

Chapter 5
   Building a Home: Richard Antone's Birth 45

Chapter 6
   6th-Grade Teacher 49

Chapter 7
   The Move to Sterling City 53

Chapter 8
   Trauma 59

Chapter 9
   Healing in Sterling City 67

Chapter 10
   Return to Red Bluff: God at Sunday Breakfast 71

Chapter 11
    1957: Sputnik and Special Ed in Red Bluff 79

Chapter 12
    Everything Changes Once Again 83

Chapter 13
    Full Circle 93

Imagination Running Wild ... short fiction 101

    Red 103

    Child of Goodness 107

    Modern Creation Myth 113

Touching the World ... thought pieces 119

    Abortion: A Legal—and Moral—Decision 121

    Colin Kaepernick 125

Missing ... and Forgetting 130

Acknowledgments 137

Life Goes On ...

... days become years

The Couple

He was an Italian boy just home from the Army.
Notice I said boy,
not man, even though he was after all twenty-two
He was a simple person, easygoing, not demanding.

She was not a girl and she was not a woman
For someone who was practically born
an adult
Of course an adultified child
She was complicated.

They met in his brother's drugstore.
He worked there.
She lived in a fifty-buck-a-month studio apartment
In the old building across the street.
They began to hang out together.
He did not pursue her.
She more than pursued him!

She had many fears laid in her lap
By the culture that informed her about all things.
What if no one wanted her?
And she never married!
After all, she was damaged goods.
She had plenty of sex.

When the first man dumped her,
She had thought,
"What's the use?"

Until her second horrible abortion
She had kept a sliver of hope.
Maybe she was wrong.
The first one was in the middle of the night.
Driving to the office blindfolded.
Her friend warning her
Do not look at the doctor.
A dark room, the only light between her legs.

The second one was legal, not because it was legal.
But with just cause, and three doctors agreeing,
And all the papers were signed.
Proving she would be mentally unfit to raise a child.
Even to survive an abortion was iffy,
in regard to her mental health.

She didn't even care.
She went home to a small town up north.
Until getting out of her friend's car,
leaving bloody smears behind her.
The doctor was called.
Another lie to her parents, a rush trip to
The city down south.

A small piece of the placenta, refusing to let go.
The doctor was relieved she had come.
If she had waited, certainly she would have died.

She seriously considered the option.
Another possibility in her life.

Now she was afraid she was a whore.
A loose woman, not a virgin.
Her mind filled with words and images
of skimpy dresses, high heels, walking the streets.
She was sure she would never get married.
She could not imagine being a well-kept mistress
or a high class prostitute.
It was beyond her experience of who she was.
There was no time to grieve; that would come later.

And there he was working in his brother's drugstore.
Freshly home from the Army.
Ripe for the picking.
She didn't even have to bat her eyelashes much
or swish her hips.
Her last hope.

He was an Italian boy just home from the Army.
Notice I said boy,
not man, even though he was after all twenty-two.
He was a simple person, easygoing, not demanding.
A good boy!

She was not a girl and she was not a woman
For someone who was practically born
an adult?
Of course, an adultified child
She was complicated.

They were married in Reno.
Sitting on a log by Lake Tahoe she looked up at him.
Oh! My God! What have I done?
She knew the answer: "Saving herself."
A baby girl was born about seven months later.
She came early, you know.
Also came the grief.

She wept when finally Roe v. Wade legalized abortion.
She wept for the children she never bore.
She wept for herself, what she had to do to save her own life.
She prayed that never again,
never again would any woman or girl
go through the fear, the self-loathing and the deep grief.
Covering the shame of not being acceptable,
not being good enough
of being ignorant and stupid.
Oh, yes, of course, mentally incompetent.

And now?
And now?
Again we may go back in time to when girls
young as fourteen thought about a wire coathanger or drinking
what was it? Was it turpentine?
Or blindfolded being driven to the dark doctor's office
late at night.
And of course being mentally incompetent.
Certainly they should not have a say
in what happens to their life
or any life.

They were married in Reno.
It was a necessary mistake.
Never to be discussed.
Her heart ached and ached, she cried and cried.

Introduction

This is no longer "my story." It is now a story of marriage and of family.

Growing up in the Harbor Gate projects in Richmond, California, in the 1940s had not given me any of the skills necessary to survive or the necessary social skills, job training, or ways to manage my money or my life. In high school I spent much of my time helping grandparents, uncles, aunts and other assorted relatives.

After high school graduation a new world began to slowly open up to me. In junior college in Redding, I learned about the theater and a much larger life than I had ever known. I learned new skills like making my own clothes, and how to dance a little. I learned a lot about drama. I also learned to set limits. I learned I could not carry 29 units of classes in spite of my efforts to prove I could.

In the early 1950s, the social options available to a young, single, working woman were severely limited by cultural and economic constraints.

Two abortions (one I almost died from) were also profoundly limiting, sobering, frightening experiences. In my usual way I believed I had only two choices: finding someone to marry me, or being a "woman of the streets." I did not believe I was glamorous enough, or skilled enough, to be a high-class "lady of the night" who lived among other "ladies of the night" and I certainly was not at all enough of anything to be a "kept lady."

Marriage seemed the only real option. Not to be someone rich or educated, but to be someone married. The influence of the culture I had grown up in limited my choice. In my Finnish family, the only choice after high school for a woman, no matter what, if she were not going to college or getting married, was to be a "working girl."

I spent the years before marriage in a variety of different situations, from living in the house on Wheeler Street in Oakland, filled with relatives, in Prineville, Oregon, to recover from severe anemia, and in the apartment on Staten Avenue with Maria or by myself. I was used to doing most things alone. Whether working at Edy's, a restaurant on Grand Avenue in Oakland, or substitute teaching, after 8 p.m. my nights were always free.

Chapter 1

Marriage and the Birth of Charlotte

My journey had been all over the place. When I quit going to the drugstore, I began to bowl and had joined what was then the Congregational Church. I also decided to go to modeling school.

My evenings were long and lonely. One day when there were no substitute teaching jobs, I decided to pick up some things at the drugstore. No one was there. I was immensely relieved. I decided the drugstore might be safe, and that I could leave if I was uncomfortable. The bar down the street was still off limits.

One of those nights a young, handsome man with black hair and brown eyes, wearing khaki pants and a T-shirt, was working behind the lunch counter. I watched Frank carefully. He seemed ordinary enough, certainly not flashy.

I began to chat with him. He was home from the Army, which he had joined after high school. His tour of duty had ended. It was not long before I began to think of him as my savior, someone I could get to marry me. As usual, I asked lots of questions. His brother was the owner of the drugstore, a pharmacist. Frank planned to go to college, become a pharmacist also, and work with his brother.

I learned in our conversations that he was one of only four White kids to graduate from the local high school. His biggest dilemma was whom to take to the prom. Frank's father cleaned out

CHAPTER 1

freight train cars for a living. The Mafia was always present in their lives, though not visible. Someone at work had once called Frank's father a Wop; that man ended up in the hospital. His dad then began to carry a gun. Frank told me about making wine in the basement. His stories did not shock me. I had my own version of those stories.

I became more interested. He had graduated from McClatchy High School in West Oakland, a very ethnically diverse neighborhood. It was considered unsafe and was a mixture of people who were on welfare, or lower class workers, or men who swept Del Monte train cars, or hauled garbage. Many were poor people not just from Italy, Spain, and France but also most other European countries. Immigrants came from all over the globe, including Mexico, Argentina, and even China.

Of course the idea of marriage to Frank began to be more appealing. Being half Finnish I understood belonging to a disenfranchised ethnic group. I also understood being part of the working class. Did I think about any of that? I doubt it. I just knew I was probably good enough until it became clear to me a Finnish non-Catholic girl probably would never be good enough for an Italian Catholic family. I actually did care very much. I believed that this might be the only opportunity I had to save myself.

It wasn't long after we started to have sex that it became obvious he had come home from the Army with an infestation of crabs. I helped him clear it up. I was angry and disappointed, yet I was still determined.

I did get pregnant and he was happy to marry me. We planned

MARRIAGE AND THE BIRTH OF CHARLOTTE

a trip to Reno where we got married in one of the small chapels that were in plentiful supply there. Frank was in slacks and a dress shirt. I wore a blue, full-skirted dress with a boat neck and big, white collar, which I had made myself. I completed my outfit with navy blue pumps and a small hat that I had decorated. Someone from the chapel stood up for us. It was not my imagined picture of "My Wedding." But it had to do.

The next day on our way home we stopped at Lake Tahoe. He owned his first Chevy, which we used for the trip. The lake was beautiful. We walked around admiring the beauty of nature. Neither of us had spent much time in the outdoors. He wanted to take my picture sitting on a log. As I sat on the log looking up at him, the first thought that not only entered my head but shocked my body, was, "Oh, my God! What have I done?"

This was not the love of my life, someone I adored. I liked him and believed I could make a life with him, and I was pregnant. And finally, I was getting married, the most acceptable thing for a young woman in her twenties to do in 1953. I was afraid of so much—being a whore, or being an old maid, no one ever wanting me. My new husband was, unbeknownst to him, my savior. A hell of a job for a young Italian guy whose family lived Old Country values.

On the way home, we talked about my converting to Catholicism and then being married in the Church. He would continue working in the drugstore and go to college, and I would substitute teach and work at Edy's.

I don't think it occurred to either of us how damned hard it was going to be. I was used to hard, but I did not know about him: he was the baby of his family. I diligently ignored that information.

He moved into my studio apartment and the Murphy bed was permanently down. It was the only place to sleep and the drop-down kitchen table never was put up again. The largest room

CHAPTER 1

was the bathroom, with its deep clawfoot bathtub. Even I could stretch out in it, all 5'8" of me.

Sometimes I would think of the guy I had dated who would come over, run a bath for me, and read me poetry as I soaked in the tub. With my new husband, it was the opposite. When he crawled into the bathtub, I would read poetry to him. I don't think he was very interested but, frankly, I didn't care. He was a good sport.

We decided to go to Red Bluff for Christmas so Frank could meet my folks. About a week before we planned to leave, my dad phoned and informed me that Mom's doctor, Dr. Wilson, wanted to meet with us. The only available time was Christmas Day. I was concerned; it seemed strange to me. My new husband visited with my mother, who was not an easy person to be with. He was cooperative and reasonably pleasant. And so was she!

Dr. Wilson informed us that my mother needed to be hospitalized as she was having a nervous breakdown. I had a flash of when I first became aware of how fragile her grasp of reality was. It was when a young woman, a student at U.C. Berkeley, was murdered, a very unusual event in those days. My mother was sure the murderer was stalking *her*. This event was a whole new anxiety. I was not very clear about what it was.

The conversation went on for a while. My three brothers were not helpful and did not want to be involved. We had another meeting. This one included the minister of the Methodist church. Her doctor explained he did not want to be involved because she might need him when she got out of Napa State Hospital for the mentally ill.

The only way we would be able to have her hospitalized without a doctor involved was to convince her to agree to being hospitalized for at least 24 hours. I may have been the only one

MARRIAGE AND THE BIRTH OF CHARLOTTE

who not only suspected but believed that in 24 hours she would be gone. I was right.

When the 24 hours were up, she was out and about. Somehow she showed up at her sister's house in Albany. I went over to talk to her, a hopeless talk. She was mentally ill, I was pretty sure, and she was also quite brilliant. Being the family scapegoat in a North Dakota Finnish farm family plainly did not help her mental wellbeing. She was at the bottom of the totem pole. Her mother did not take care of her children's needs.

The Methodist minister and my dad drove her back to Napa. I went back to Oakland with my husband. I spent the next few months tracking her down to get her help. I went to my aunt's to visit her. The next day she caught the train to Los Gatos, where her other sister was. Both my dad and I followed her there, and then up to Crescent City.

After Crescent City, my doctor plainly told me, "No more." I was done. I went to my apartment and waited for two things: the birth of my baby, and where my mother would be going next. The baby wasn't eager to appear on the scene, and my mother headed to Oregon. My dad was on his own and so was I, but I didn't know this yet.

The baby did not arrive on her due date. I had left Edy's before the due date, with an illustrious bassinet. Eighteen others had used this bassinet, some of them quite famous, like the speaker of the California House of Representatives. My maternity wardrobe had consisted of clothes donated by my fellow waitresses, plus two outfits from my new mother-in-law. She had worn them when she was expecting my husband. She warned me to only go out at night so I wouldn't be seen. She also gave me ten yards of white flannel she had bought at the Tenth Street Market when she was expecting Frank, twenty-plus years ago. I used every bit of it making clothes for the baby, due any day now.

CHAPTER 1

The saga with my mother continued until there was a sanity hearing in Oregon in which she was declared legally sane. My dad returned to Red Bluff feeling defeated, a way-too-familiar state for him, and one I knew well. I had listened to him over the many years when he was either defeated or guilty. Soon he found a new woman and focused his attentions on her.

It wasn't long before the baby began to make her presence known. The doctor who delivered her had his practice at East Oakland Hospital. I suppose what I remember best about him were the seven times he stuck me to get blood, after which I went across the street to have coffee, feeling a little weird. I barely made it without fainting.

When I actually went into labor, I don't remember how I got to the hospital. The baby was already two weeks late. In some strange way I understood her reluctance to be born. Frank never showed up. The next day, when new grandmothers typically came to see their daughters and grandchildren, I felt unbelievably lonely. No one showed up to see my beautiful daughter or me. Finally, Frank showed up to meet his eight-pound daughter, Charlotte Jean—the name he had chosen for her.

Chapter 2

Oakland: Adjusting to Marriage

My apartment was too small for our new family, so we began to look for another place close to the drugstore and Edy's. I remember during this time, that when Frank had told his brother about our marriage, his response was, "What did you do that for? She has already worn out four men." Funny, I wished I had known their names since I never recalled any of them. Then there was his mother's response, "Who ever heard of an Italian marrying a Finn?" Ethnic pride was strong.

Charlotte was not a happy new resident of this planet. She was fussy, colicky, and cried and cried. I worked when Frank was home and he watched her. He had never been around a baby. I got a bottle ready for her before work and knew, if she fussed enough, he would feed her. Changing diapers was another story. I would come home to a screaming, wet baby, with her father sometimes holding her while he watched TV. He is not to be blamed, nor was I. In his family, the men conceived children and then ignored them until they were active. In my family, my mother's two brothers abandoned their daughters. My own father barely knew any of us. He was often angry at my brothers and used me to

CHAPTER 2

confess what a bad man he was himself. He wasn't bad; none of them were. They were all shaped by their culture.

While we lived in the small apartment, I washed clothes by hand, carried them up two flights of stairs, and hung them on a clothesline to dry. When they were dry, I took them down, carried them downstairs and put them away.

Finally, we found an upstairs apartment—more of a duplex, since there were only two units in the building. In the small bedroom we set up Charlotte's crib and chest of drawers. It was heaven. She was in the only bedroom off the living room. We had the dining room. We put up an old iron bed with three mattresses my mother-in-law had given us. I could put a finger on top and one underneath the three and feel my finger through all three layers of mattresses.

The best addition to our possessions was an electric wringer washing machine. I was thrilled to have the washer even though I carried the laundry down a flight of stairs to the neighbor's clotheslines. On wash day, I pulled the machine next to the sink and washed clothes. Not like Alicia did, my grandfather's wife, who washed her clothes, turned them inside-out, washed them again, and rinsed them in the same way, but good enough!

Hanging clothes on the clothesline was the way I met my Mormon neighbor who had a large family and a husband I never saw during the time I lived in the building. She lived in the next building and was currently pregnant. We became a comfort for each other, she with her large brood and me with my very first child. I had never met a Mormon before and I learned a lot about her and what it meant to be a Mormon.

Next door to me lived an older couple. Yvonne was from the South and Sam was an executive in a big corporation. She offered to watch Charlotte and there were times when I took her up on it. I was glad they lived across the small back porch.

OAKLAND: ADJUSTING TO MARRIAGE

Her husband Sam walked to work every morning except Saturday and Sunday. It was obvious that he tucked a pint inside his jacket. Yvonne was the first White woman I had met from the South and her husband the first executive I had ever met. I was intrigued. They also became helpful friends. They loved Charlotte and willingly watched her while I ran an errand or something. I was grateful they lived next door since I was never sure if Frank could really take care of Charlotte. I knew Yvonne, or even staggering Sam, could and would help. When Charlotte was with her dad, I came home from work way too often to a baby with a soaking wet diaper.

I loved my conversations with Sam and Yvonne. They ranged from corporate America to living in the South with deep racial tensions. Yvonne often swore she was not at all prejudiced. The Black people worked for her family and all she asked was that they stay in their place, like never come into the living room unless asked, and other examples. I never challenged her. I was curious how she got to where she was in her thinking. As time went on, Sam and Yvonne both slurred their speech more and staggered a little more.

Every Sunday, Frank went to his mother's for breakfast. If I wasn't working, I would go. If I was working, he would take Charlotte.

The house was an old Victorian in West Oakland, now old and run down. Frank had lived there all of his life. He was what was called a change-of-life baby. He was conceived sometime close to or during menopause. His brother and sister were twenty years older than he was and had their own families.

The house was full to spilling over. There was a newspaper path from the front door to the kitchen. Surrounding the path was everything from a round table filled with boxes of chocolates, fancy dishes, and tins of cookies, to a china cabinet stacked full

CHAPTER 2

and piled high.

What had been Frank's bedroom, the parlor off the entry, was still his bedroom. I am almost positive his mother wished he might come home again.

Now there was a highchair in the kitchen. I think every time we visited Frank's mother, Josephine pinched Charlotte's nose—so it would not spread all over her face—and reminded me to wipe her face with one of her wet diapers so she would be beautiful.

I would watch Josephine bend over the wood-burning stove stirring a pot of food that I was never quite sure was edible—things like chicken heads, chicken feet, or some other part of an animal that I had never known anyone to eat. She wanted me to learn how to make ravioli, a two-day project involving brains and spinach. I was not at all enthusiastic.

In the garden/back yard were chickens that kept the family in eggs. I watched her boil eggs, turn off the flame and wait barely a minute before she lifted them out with her bare hands. I was shocked.

There was always wine that they made in their basement. In a huge barrel the wine was fermented to the state's specifications as to strength. The maximum acceptable strength was 13% alcohol. They weren't careful, but only got caught once and paid a fine.

The chickens roamed the back yard, which was full of vegetables: chard, spinach, parsley, and other plants I did not recognize. We left for home with a chicken—not a fryer or a young chicken, but a chicken so old the skin was like leather and the bones bleached white in places. Graciously, I thanked her, while inside I was swearing like a longshoreman.

During that time we contacted the priest in the little Catholic church facing Lake Merritt on upper Lakeshore Avenue. We wanted to take care of the commitment that I become Catholic before Charlotte could be baptized. I took instructions in Catholicism under the tutelage of the priest, who always looked a little grim. After I was baptized, both of us were instructed on the marriage vows. We were married in the priest's office and that Sunday I received my first Holy Communion.

As I knelt at the altar with the soles of my feet facing the congregation, I was embarrassed and self-conscious. I was used to wearing shoes with big holes in the soles and cardboard inside to cover the holes, but I was quite certain no one sitting in the pews facing the altar, all middle-class, well-dressed Catholics, had ever experienced wearing shoes with soles almost gone.

Charlotte was baptized in the family's Catholic church, and Frank's brother, owner of the drugstore, and his wife stood up as her godparents. My immediate family had no religious affiliation, in spite of my Finnish grandfather's family who were members of a very strict Lutheran sect who did not believe in doctors, music (except hymns), dancing, makeup, pretty clothes, playing, or fun. They believed in God, hard work, and avoiding anything that even hinted of sin. Two of his sisters died because of their refusal to see a doctor. They believed my grandfather and his wife—especially his wife—were headed for Hell.

I was pretty sure that in the minds of my Protestant relatives, joining the Catholic Church sealed my fate. I only knew one of the sisters well. I saw her at every holiday at my grandfather's house where she would say "grace," praying for all of us for at least thirty minutes—unless my grandfather said "Amen" after twenty minutes.

Being accepted in either world was a challenge, especially after I told my uncles that if they ever teased Charlotte like they had teased me, they would only see her once. They did not un-

CHAPTER 2

derstand. I could not explain it, but I knew what it was like being told, as they laughed, that I looked like Eleanor Roosevelt, the homeliest woman in the world, or the number of other ways they had teased me or made fun of me.

No one had heard from my mother until my dad had a new woman in his life. How she knew was a mystery. And suddenly, my parents were back together again. The two of them were connected in ways that were not at all understandable. The way hate turned to love and the pendulum swung back and forth seemed strange and marvelous at the same time. She did not see her first grandchild until Charlotte was four months old. I never knew what to expect from either of my parents. On a trip we took to Red Bluff they were pleasantly delighted with Charlotte and I was so relieved I could not find another emotion, just cautious relief.

One of the things that broke my heart was finding out my husband was not attending Contra Costa Junior College to become a pharmacist, but was going to the horse races. My dreams began to crumble, to fall apart. Yet I knew I absolutely had to hang on and make the necessary adjustments to make our life work.

Chapter 3

Red Bluff: Beth's Birth in Oakland

Our life continued in a well-established pattern of work, family, and not much entertainment but holiday celebrations. Charlotte grew, and looked beautiful in a wardrobe of hand-me-downs from the Jewish family who came into Edy's and befriended me in many ways. Their hand-me-downs started with Charlotte, went to my niece Rhonda, to my second daughter Beth, and then to Karen, Rhonda's sister.

I disliked substitute teaching. Once I substituted in a second-grade class in an elementary school in West Oakland. There was a seven-year-old child who, when he saw me, never quit screaming or running around the room. His teacher had created a relationship with him that kept him sane; a substitute terrified him. I called the office and had him removed. He was gone and the quiet was amazing. In ten minutes he showed up at the door and we started over. This time I took him to the office and announced, "If he stays, I leave." The situation was not good for anyone. There was no adequate plan for him and certainly no resources to help him settle into his classrooms. Watching him, I was able to recognize his fear, despair and anger. He was lost and only his teacher could help him. No one else knew how to reach him. Including me.

In one school I kept a fifth-grade Black girl after school who informed me her big sister was going to come to school and stab me.

CHAPTER 3

"You have fifteen more minutes. Please sit at your desk."

As she stood there I announced, "For every minute you stand there, I will add two minutes."

I went back to my desk to work. Finally, she went to her desk, and after about five minutes, I told her she could leave. She left; I never saw her sister.

The gap between what I was learning in my Education classes and what was happening in public school was like a giant sinkhole. When I was doing my student teaching, I was placed in a fourth-grade class in Oakland where the teacher regularly hit kids across their outstretched palm with a ruler. I thought she was rare until I substituted and learned she was not the exception but the rule.

I remember one student I caught doing something who pleaded with me, "Please, Teacher, don't hit me," over and over again as he crouched and covered his hand. The Crusader in me made a commitment that I would change all of this when I had my own classroom. Little did I know.

I did begin reading everything I could find about child development. I was fortunate to have had a wonderful pediatrician, Dr. Fisher, the first year of Charlotte's life. He charged $60 for the entire year. Every year it would go up a little. When I expressed concern about her having a pacifier, he looked at me and stated, "I have never had a patient that still had a pacifier when they started school or if they did, they only used it at home."

When I was concerned about toilet training, his response was "When she is twenty years old, I don't think anyone will care or ask her how old she was when she was toilet trained."

I believe we still need this kind of pediatrician.

RED BLUFF: BETH'S BIRTH IN OAKLAND

It soon became clear to me that Frank would never leave his $50-a-week job at the drugstore. Things began to come to a head when someone decided to tell me that the girl who worked on the lunch counter was pregnant, and Frank was the father!

I told her, "That may be true, but he will always park his shoes under my bed."

That ended the conversation. That night I confronted Frank. I told him what I heard and announced that if it was true, he had a responsibility to help support the child and take care of the child, and if she didn't want the baby, we were responsible for providing a home for the child. He totally denied it. What was true? Who knows?

At about this time, Diamond National Lumber Company opened a new mill in Red Bluff. One of my parents told Frank about it and suggested he ought to apply for a job at the new mill. Someone told me about it and suggested the same thing. Returning to Red Bluff did not hold much appeal, but neither did Sundays at his mother's house and holidays at his brother's house. I saw no future for myself at Edy's or as a teacher, and I saw less future for Frank at the drugstore without a degree in pharmacy. I was also expecting my second child. I did not see how we would handle childcare.

Frank did apply for the job, and he got one—the lowest level job in a mill, working on the green chain. He got ready to start work.

When I told my doctor of our new plan, he said there was no way I could make such a move in the middle of my pregnancy.

CHAPTER 3

I told Frank I could not move until after the baby's September due date. It was then late July. This seemed manageable.

I talked to my uncle and aunt and made arrangements to stay with them until the baby was born, but there was no room with them for Charlotte. In a conversation with my neighbor Yvonne about our dilemma, she suggested that we let Charlotte go to Red Bluff with her dad. She knew someone who could go with them and take care of her.

We had a plan: Charlotte would go with Frank to Red Bluff and they would live in my parents' house. Ruth, the Black woman Yvonne knew, agreed to go and stay until I could go to Red Bluff with the new baby. Frank had also rented a small house where we stored our stuff. We planned to move into the house after the new baby arrived.

I insisted that no one bring Charlotte to see me during this time. I believed visiting and leaving, over and over again, would not only be way too hard on her, it would also be very difficult for both of us. I was not sure I could let her go. What made it possible were the stories reported to me about Ruth's care for her. Charlotte was her number one priority and if asked to do other tasks, she refused, responding, "I came here to care for Charlotte."

Ruth was, to my knowledge, the only Black woman in Red Bluff. I still feel deep gratitude, love and appreciation for her. She loved Charlotte and took beautiful care of her. I think Charlotte survived and grew well because of Ruth.

September twenty-third, the baby's due date, came and went. October twenty-third passed by also. Finally, on November twenty-second, there was some evidence she might be born. She waited until November twenty-third and was born in the early morning with lots of help. It seemed none of my babies were excited to be on this planet. Frank had chosen Charlotte's name and now it was my turn: Elizabeth Ann, also known as Beth or Beth Ann. Smaller than her sister and more determined, she entered the world.

Again, I was alone in the hospital with no one from my family there.

Chapter 4

Settling into Red Bluff: Work and Family

When I got out of the hospital after Frank arrived in Oakland, we went to my aunt and uncle's house. Arlene, my aunt, was Native American, from a tribe in the Monterey area. She was quiet, helpful, and kind. She was also a slow mover. Dinner was often after nine p.m. and she cooked whatever her kids said they wanted. I liked her a lot; she was helpful to me. We stayed with Arlene and my Uncle Norval.

The next morning, we packed up our belongings and headed to Red Bluff. Everyone was waiting for us—my parents, Ruth and Charlotte, and my three brothers, Elvin, Charles, and Roy.

The day after we arrived we learned that the woman who owned the house Frank had rented decided not to rent it to us. I knew we could not stay with my parents forever. I wanted Ruth to stay, but she was ready to go home. The following day we began to look for a house. I still did not know how to drive. Once I tried to learn while my brothers laughed at and teased me. I think maybe two of them lived at home at that time.

We finally found a house south of Red Bluff. There were two bedrooms. It reminded me of the projects.

Frank worked graveyard shift. Money was tight. I was a wreck. Frank would go to work at 11 p.m. and get home around 5 or 6 a.m., eat something, have a beer or two, and finally go to bed at

CHAPTER 4

about the time I got up in the morning. He slept most of the day, then went to work.

I was alone in a strange house with a toddler and a new baby, and I was exhausted. When it rained, the rugs would be soaking wet. When it did not rain, the rugs were full of black ants, which I vacuumed up every morning. I did not understand the flooding. After much observation, seeing how the water lay on the land, I decided the sewer line was broken and that the water rising up through the floor was from the sewer.

I called my dad to check. My dad agreed with my assessment. Frank did not have a clue. I called the Health Department and they made it clear they would not do anything. Neither would anyone in Public Works. The owners of the property had a lot more political power than I did. We began looking for another house. Christmas came. We had no money. I was hanging on by a thread. My parents bought gifts for my kids, and I was grateful beyond measure.

Out of desperation I looked up a friend from college and another woman I had known. We made arrangements to meet. I got a ride into town to meet them. I had kept contact with them the best I could.

I was functioning, but not very well. I was barely able to hold onto something that kept me going. In my mind we had to move. The problems with the house made it dangerous for our children and probably for us also. I moved from anger to fear, back and forth, over and over again.

Finally, my parents' next door neighbors came and asked where we were. They planned to move and they wondered if we wanted to rent their house, right next door to my parents. It was built after the Second World War to accommodate returning veterans. Housing projects similar to this one were all over America; on the coasts, in valley towns, prairie towns, desert towns.

They were everywhere. There was a similarity about all of them. The floor plans were all the same: two or three small bedrooms, one bathroom, living room, small dining room and kitchen which opened onto the garage with a utility sink and a back door to the yard. It was better than any place I had lived for a very long time. All the rugs we had brought from Oakland were ruined, but the bare floors were quite beautiful and somewhat fragile.

It was a home, a real home.

We settled in with our few possessions and we furnished the house with hand-me-downs, mostly from family. We also got homemade Italian sausage in the mail regularly from Frank's mother. We would open the package, Frank would clean the mold off the casings, and we would store it in the refrigerator. It was a stretch for me to accept that once the casings were cleaned with vinegar, the sausage was perfectly fine to eat. We had many culture clashes between the Finns and the Italians.

I had not learned to drive so I walked everywhere, pushing a stroller holding the two girls. In order not to be isolated, I joined a group called Crib Age, a women's group for new mothers. I stood in the kitchen listening to a conversation about the best way to wash dishes—I must say a conversation that I had no interest in joining—or a conversation about who walked first, or what children were already toilet trained and which ones still had a ways to go. As I listened, I learned one important thing: toilet training was achieved when the mother was well-trained in knowing the signs of a need for the bathroom. I became even less interested. I did not last long as a member of the Crib Age group. Soon I decided it was not for me.

Frank still worked the graveyard shift, but it was not long before he changed to the day shift. Like most couples in the fifties, our communication still left a lot to be desired. When my mother complained about my father all the time I was growing

CHAPTER 4

up, and continued to complain almost until he died, I would remind her that maybe she had a part in it. Of course, I knew I had a part in it. Neither Frank nor I had any idea how to communicate.

A time that stands out for me was when I wanted to take the two girls for a ride. It was Sunday and he would not budge. I decided I was not going to sit around the house one more day. I put the girls in a stroller, crowded together, and stormed out of the house, planning to walk downtown. I was used to walking. A five-mile walk was not hard for me, but pushing a stroller with two toddlers in it was. I did walk downtown and then home. I was not in a happy mood. I had no way to communicate my exhaustion, my hurt feeling, and feelings of not being loved or cared about. I had experienced these feelings all my life. I did not expect to feel anything else. I glared at Frank—still in bed—took the girls out of the stroller and put them down for a nap. I sat in the living room and seethed.

We settled into life in Red Bluff. Frank was promoted and now worked in the warehouse; I took a teaching job and the girls went to the "Teachers' Day Care." It was so called because the owner's daughter was a teacher, and it was also the day care used by every teacher I knew. My reading material at that time was about child development, parenting and education. I did not have much company in my choice of reading.

I think my classroom was the only one where students did not sit quietly in rows. When the principal evaluated me, he had no complaints about my teaching, but he did have complaints about my messy desk. I was very confused as well as relieved.

We lived in the house next door to my parents until Charlotte was four or five, and Beth two years younger. The two sisters were so different from each other, and I was delighted by them.

Chapter 5

Building a Home: Richard Antone's Birth

We had heard about a builder who was highly respected and we decided to build our first house. We met with the builder; he had a lot available in Antelope on a little street at the end of the road next to the fairgrounds. In July I was taking swimming lessons while we planned to build a new house. At the lesson I announced I was pregnant. When someone asked how far along I was, my response was nine hours and fifty minutes. The truth is I was quite accurate about the timing. The group of women learning to swim enjoyed my response and we all laughed together.

I made one thing clear to Frank and to my mother: I expected them both to be there or available in some way. I was not doing this pregnancy and birth alone!

Our son was born close to the time the house was finished. I had taken a leave from my job and liked my new doctor, Dr. Merhoff. My pregnancy was easy. All three of my pregnancies were easy.

What was not easy was the birth.

None of my children were very willing to be born. Every one of them was born after their due date. With my third pregnancy, a very big, over-ten-pound boy was born closest to his due date. His was baptized Richard Antone. Frank's boss Ed Casey and his wife, good Irish Catholics, were his godparents.

CHAPTER 5

We had moved into our new home shortly after his birth, and we began to settle into the house. I had taken a leave for the rest of the school year, planning to return in September. This time my mother provided money to pay for help; she was working. Frank was available, but was he helpful? It just wasn't part of his culture. In fact, men helping out with the children was not yet a part of American culture.

I loved the house and considered myself blessed to have it. It was a simple house, maybe 1800 square feet, built on a short, dead-end street. There were four houses facing the street and two houses facing the road along the fairgrounds.

Our house had features which were not yet popular: a dining room that opened to the living room, sliding glass doors off the dining room, and a family room. The floors were parquet hardwood—beautiful floors. The double drapes for the dining room and living room were a soft rose color. When they were closed, the room was a dark rose. When the heavy drapes were open and the sheer drapes closed, the room had a soft pink glow. And when everything was open the two rooms were bright with light. The house had only one bathroom, which was standard, and the laundry was in the garage. I made all the drapes and curtains for the house, turquoise with white rickrack trim and pink-checkered for the girls' room, and white drapes on the sheer side.

Richard Antone entered the world slowly. The doctor, rather than giving me a drug to help the birth, massaged the birth canal until the baby decided to push into this world. He was an easy baby. When he was four months old, he went to the babysitter's and Charlotte started school at the Catholic school.

Charlotte entered kindergarten with fifty-nine other children. I was beside myself. I was so angry, I could not believe it. I worked at being a good Catholic and it was hard. I finally decided Confession was a pretty worthless practice for me. My greatest sin was using birth control, and I knew I was not going to quit. Knowing that, I saw no point in going to Confession. I loved the rituals of the church but was most often bored by the services. Furthermore, I could not really forgive them for a sixty-child kindergarten and my efforts to change it were met consistently with denial that it was a problem. I was sure it was the only time any of my children would attend a Catholic school, but I was wrong.

The house was beginning to take shape and become a home. The neighborhood was a strange mix. On one side of me lived a local pharmacist and his family. His wife, who had the same first name as I did, Beverly, was a known social climber. We belonged to the same group of young couples. I had known one of these young couples before they married. Activities with them were the core of our social life. Beverly lived in chronic dissatisfaction and certainly let me know that the living situation was way beneath her.

Next door on the other side was a new family who had just moved into the neighborhood. Their son and my oldest daughter became fast friends, to the point where they were inseparable. It was curious to me, since in our last house she and the boy across the street were similarly inseparable. First thing in the morning, she would put on her dad's heavy fatigue jacket—winter, summer, spring or fall—and rush out of the house to find Timothy. I don't think either of them even thought about food.

During one hot Red Bluff summer, my middle child, Beth, found a mud hole in the neighbor's garden and lay in it to cool off. The neighbor came to get me. There was my muddy daughter, enjoying herself.

Another way the children were totally different was around bedtime. Charlotte, sometime between 8 and 8:30, would announce she wanted to go to bed and she would, while Beth would go to bed at nine or later, where she still played in her crib, talking and singing. One night she climbed onto the chest of drawers

CHAPTER 5

at the end of her bed, trying to get to the floor. She pulled the dresser down on top of herself. Both of us rushed to get her and squeezed in through the door to help her. She was not hurt, but after that the dresser was moved, never to return to the old place at the end of her crib.

Charlotte did not care what she wore. Usually, she wore her dad's Army hat, his Army jacket and shorts, rain or shine, sunny or freezing.

Beth, on the other hand, cared very much about what she wore.

When I took them shopping, I would pick out three items for them so they could choose which they wanted. Charlotte wasn't interested in any of them. She just grabbed one. But Beth didn't like any of them, and she went back to the rack and picked an outfit herself. I was pretty sure it would look awful on her, but I was wrong! It looked much better on her than what I had chosen. From then on, it was about what each of them chose. Char: shorts, long pants, and maybe an old T-shirt. Beth: an outfit she found on the dress rack, and it was always perfect.

In the summer I tried to get Char out of her dad's Army jacket. No luck!

Chapter 6

6th-Grade Teacher

I went back to teaching in September, this time to teach sixth grade at a different elementary school, Jackson Heights, in Red Bluff.

I had read enough about children and education to take some risks. There were no male sixth-grade teachers and the principal could not find anyone to coach the sixth-grade football team for the inter-school league. Finally, I volunteered. I went home and read the whole section in the encyclopedia about football, coming away both surprised and pleased. It was not a game of brawn necessarily, but a game of strategy and working together.

We played flag football. I could not wear slacks to coach or to the games. I wore a skirt. It was close the end of the '50s, but nothing had yet changed. We had won every game and now we were playing our very last game against Antelope School. We lost. Everyone was disappointed, including me. In the back of the van, the son of the high school basketball coach sat punching his fist. "If we only had a man coach, we would have won."

I turned slightly toward him and said, "You just flunked PE."

He replied, "You can't do that!"

And I said, "I might be able to do exactly that, but I won't."

To this day, I still believe flag football is a better game than tackle.

CHAPTER 6

In the classroom, we did a nutrition study with white rats. We had two cages. One cage was assigned healthy food and the other, unhealthy food. The experiment ended when one of the students took them home for the weekend and mixed them up in the cages. Accidentally, I hoped. I also hoped he did not mix up the sexes, but he did. He was a smart kid and I always suspected maybe it was deliberate. Soon we had sixteen baby rats to care for, feed, and help to keep alive. Probably most died. I suppose there were more important lessons in that event than I even knew.

We started a company and sold stocks. At lunch and after school we sold candy bars, marked up a couple of cents or a nickel. We kept track of the stock, the cost, and the profit.

I was not very good at spelling. One time I misspelled a word and a girl in the class caught it. She was so pleased with herself. I asked her to show me in a dictionary. From that day forward I made a regular practice of misspelling words. Every person in my class had their dictionary out waiting for a misspelled word. I loved it. On the overhead projector I would put something students wrote from an assignment. The class read it, looked for spelling, punctuation, and grammar mistakes, and evaluated the quality of the paper. No one ever knew whose paper it was. The results were a surprise. Everyone's writing improved, including mine.

I also gave an assignment to different members of the class to write word problems. It was a homework assignment. I would collect them, have someone write numbers on the blackboard. First task was asking if it was a problem that could be solved. How good was the presentation? If they were stumped, and the problem was solvable but did not get solved, the writer of the word problem received a prize.

We also talked about stars and I asked them to look for different constellations. We decided to build a telescope. I ordered the pieces, and we put it together. I think everyone in the class participated. What was lacking was a stand for the telescope that allowed it to turn 360 degrees around, as well as up and down. We all tried. The principal came into the classroom and tried. I suggested they take the puzzle home and work on it there. Almost everyone in the class took it home. Weeks went by, and one day I arrived at school to find a student waiting for me with his parents. They had been up all night working on the problem. They had been at school waiting for me since 6 a.m. They didn't even let me open the classroom before they began to explain, "We have solved the problem!"

I checked their design, the principal checked it, and we agreed. It seemed they had solved it. I don't remember ever seeing a family as excited.

Everyone went to my classroom and took out the telescope and watched as the father put it together. I will tell you, when he demonstrated it we all cheered. Right then the class began to plan a stargazing party which we held in the parking lot and invited all parents, the School Board superintendent, and any teacher who wanted to attend. None did. Building that telescope with the class is still one of my highlights as a teacher. It was that year when a teacher confronted me in the hall and informed me I needed to stop, to slow down—I was making the other teachers look bad. I told him that wasn't in my power.

We were studying the Aztecs and the class wanted to put on a play. A girl in the class wrote the play. It was not assigned, she just wrote it. In the play there was a scene of the human sacrifice of a young virgin. I had gotten a lamb's heart from a local meatpacking plant. During the play the high priest appeared to be cutting out the heart from the virgin and held it up to the sky, to the gods. Every student in the school who saw this scene loved it.

We also published a monthly newspaper. And my class also

CHAPTER 6

put on the Christmas play. Another sixth-grade teacher did the music and worked with the choir.

The School Board superintendent thought I was fabulous. I loved teaching and loved my class. I heard one of the boys in that class ended up in prison, and I am still saddened by the story.

I actually don't remember anyone having the kind of classroom I had unless the school provided a teacher's aide and provided extra money for supplies. Many a night I was up until midnight.

Chapter 7

The Move to Sterling City

During this time, Frank got a promotion to be office manager in Sterling City. Sterling City is not a city. It is the name of a dying timber town that was revived as a stud mill. There was not much there. Frank moved up to Sterling City while I stayed in Red Bluff to sell the house, teach for maybe three months, and get ready to move. My big task was to learn to drive. We had a yellow and black 1959 Chevy with what looked like wings. It was a very popular, in-demand car. We moved to Sterling City some time in the early '60s.

I barely learned to drive, but I did learn. We packed up the house, sold it and left Red Bluff. Our house in Sterling City was not ready so we rented another. Now, Sterling City was a surprise. There was a Forestry station, the Diamond Lumber Mill, an abandoned—or mostly abandoned—hotel, a small post office/market, a small restaurant, and a bar. That was the entire town.

Up the hill a bit was the Community Hall. For almost a hundred years the most important function there was a big gathering and feast for hunters who stopped for the annual event in Sterling City. On the very top of the hill at the end of town was the school, housing kindergarten to eighth grade in three classrooms: kindergarten and first in one room, second to fourth in another room, and fifth to eighth grades in the third.

CHAPTER 7

Both my daughters started school there, in September.

We went to Paradise to buy groceries and anything else we needed. We made the trip once a week. There may have been a little church on a side street. It was most likely a Pentecostal church. A small group met on Sunday morning in the community hall. We drove down the hill for Sunday mass.

Finally, we moved into our house. We paid $60 a month. It had been a company house and the home of the mill supervisor. His wife was probably the only woman in town who wore a dress, hat, and sturdy pumps to work in the yard. The community talked about her in awe. They were long gone since the mill had closed.

Again, I made curtains and used what I could from our Red Bluff house. I bought priscillas for the living room, and a braided rug. I bought living room furniture, for the first time buying my own. It was early American, stained to look like maple. The house had an upstairs, where the girls had two rooms, one with twin beds and dressers and the other a toy room. We warned them sternly about what to do in case of fire, which was always a threat.

The people working for Diamond banded together to create a community. The forester and his family joined us. His father was head of California Forestry. We got together on a regular basis.

I started playing bridge. One couple retired to Sterling City from the Bay Area. She had worked at I. Magnin in San Francisco. Playing bridge with them was where I learned the saying, "Breast your cards." It became part of my bridge vocabulary. We also played with the new young forester and his wife.

All my brothers worked for either Cal Forestry or US Forestry. My youngest brother worked for the state until he reached retirement age. My middle brother went to Humboldt State and got his degree in forestry. The oldest of my three brothers, fifteen months younger than me, went into the insurance business. Most conversations in my young adult years were about problems with the forest and fires. Everyone had strong opinions about the best plans for the forest.

Frank's boss and his wife and daughter visited often. I remember the Thanksgiving we forgot to take the paper bag out of the turkey, filled with the liver, heart and other goodies. Or the time their daughter and Beth were playing upstairs and their daughter came running downstairs shouting, "Beth needs you!"

Frank ran up the stairs and I ran outside. Beth was hanging from the upstairs window! Frank pulled her safely into the house.

Charlotte, Beth, and Tony were all adventurous children. Charlotte got stuck in a hunting blind at the top of a pine tree. Tony went walking almost every day, when he was no more than three or four years old, from the bottom of town to the top of town, where the Brakehill house was located, to visit "Brakie," as he called him. Mr. Brakehill was the principal at the school where I taught, Sterling City Elementary School.

One of our biggest adventures was when Charlotte found a rattlesnake curled up under a box she had lifted up. She came home and told us. Frank took a shovel and ended the rattlesnake's life—the snake had ten rattles.

I had never driven in the snow. The first winter I slid off the road into a ditch. Then I slid into a snowbank. I switched back to walking. At least I knew how to walk.

After the girls started school, a parent who had a son in the first grade approached me in the grocery store/post office.

"Did you know that Miss Cartwheel is telling the little boys that if they read well, they can kiss Beth?" I could not, did not, believe it until Beth confirmed the story. The next day I was waiting for Miss Cartwheel in her kindergarten classroom. This was among the many things that surprised me about Sterling City.

CHAPTER 7

Eventually I taught second, third and fourth grades. Charlotte may have been in my class. Teaching in Sterling City was a different cup of tea from teaching in Oakland or Red Bluff. There was a very small staff. The principal, Mr. Brakehill, had been the only principal the school ever had. He and his wife and daughter lived in the last house in town, across from the school. Their daughter, Marilyn, was our babysitter, and we all loved her—all my kids, me, and Frank. She was a joy to have in our lives. I still have fond memories of her and would love to see her.

One of my projects for my class was making a book about each of their families. They dictated all of their family stories and I printed them for the book. They drew and colored pictures of their family. I drew a portrait of them and wrote the story about them. Parents loved them and they became keepsakes for many of the families.

Winters in Sterling City were particularly hard. Often the school would close when the roads were too slick and icy to drive. The flume broke or froze on a regular basis. When that happened, there was no water. The problem was Diamond's responsibility and everyone who worked at Diamond drove to the flume, found a place to collect water, and drove it to town to deliver it. My son was in diapers and the scarcity of water made it impossible to keep up with the diapers and family laundry. The foresters, the boss at the stud mill, Frank and anyone else who was available helped haul water. I was exhausted, as was everyone.

We got together at different houses to cook and heat one house enough to stay warm. In every house there was a wood stove in the kitchen and a heater in the living room, all quite old. Heating all the houses was definitely a chore.

We settled into our minimalist life in Sterling City, made friends, socialized. In Butte Meadows, up in the mountains, we had an old, beat-up cabin which was owned by Diamond. When we went to the cabin, Frank and my dad would work on it. It needed everything—stoves for the kitchen and for heat, windows to replace broken, cracked and disappearing ones. The bathroom needed to be rebuilt, and all the fixtures needed to be replaced. My parents would visit. We slept on the floor which meant sleeping on snow. The wind blew under us, over us and around us. It was a cold winter, but we had lots of blankets.

The kids loved it. They could roam, explore, run and climb with almost complete abandon. Charlotte's friend Carmen from school came to Butte Meadows in the summer. Her family owned the bar/restaurant/grocery store in Sterling City.

Chapter 8

Trauma

My mother and her brother Harold were two of the brightest in a very bright family. When Harold was drafted, the Army trained him in intelligence because he was too brilliant to be a foot soldier. From his very brief marriage after the war, he had a daughter, Kathy. He abandoned her and her mother Alice and never saw them again until Kathy was ten years old. He never paid child support; never spent a nickel on her.

When Alice died, Harold had been contacted. He needed to find a home for his daughter. Kathy had a halfsister, Sharon, living in Las Vegas. When Sharon was twelve, Alice packed her up and dumped her at her father's house. Later, when Alice was part of our family, her stories about Sharon's father were grim. She indicated he was an alcololic, violent, capable of murder and, in general, an evil man.

Sharon was never protected from these stories. Nevertheless, she was willing to provide a home for her half-sister. My Uncle Harold had asked all his sisters to offer Kathy a home, and when none volunteered, he asked me. I was the last one from Kathy's family that I knew of and I hadn't seen Sharon since she was a child. But I could not bear the thought of a foster home for Kathy, nor of her living with Sharon's allegedly evil father. I agreed to meet with the attorney.

CHAPTER 8

A decision was made that Sharon would come to visit me, bringing Kathy. They would stay a week, then go to Las Vegas for a week. Meanwhile, it would be decided what to do.

When they arrived, Kathy immediately joined my daughters. Sharon was a mess, seriously depressed, her marriage was falling apart. Her two sons were acting out and her life was in shambles. Every night for a week I sat up and listened to her, learning how terribly troubled she was and the ways she had been deeply, psychically wounded. She was hanging on by a very frayed thread. Being dumped at her dad's as a child actually turned out to be the best thing that had happened to her. It wasn't great, but it was definitely less toxic for her than before.

Although alcoholic, my Uncle Harold, at the end of the week, drove them to Reno to catch a bus to Las Vegas. I stayed home, feeling the tragedy of the situation, exhausted and knowing Sharon could not care for Kathy.

In the end, Kathy did come to live with us that summer.

It was during this summer that one day Carmen, whose family lived in Sterling City in the winter and who owned the Butte Meadows bar, restaurant, and grocery store, came to me. She was solemn. "Charlotte has something to tell you." And indeed she did!

Charlotte, who was ten years old, could barely talk. A local eighteen-year-old, who was limited intellectually and emotionally, had raped her. I knew him, since he had been in my class when I taught fifth through eighth grades. He didn't hit or beat her or tear her clothes off. He simply raped her.

By this time, I had handled so much I now suspect I thought I could handle anything, but perhaps the rest of my family could not. If it had not been for a friend in Red Bluff and my brother's wife June, I am not sure I would have survived that summer.

I was deeply devastated and felt strongly that somehow I had failed my daughter. I called the police, knowing the family and the young man's history, because I wanted him to get help and the only way I knew for that to happen was to involve the law. When I contacted the only officer in Sterling City and expressed my intentions, he didn't agree or disagree. He just did his job—the minimally acceptable effort.

I was very different from most of the people in Sterling City. Most of them were loggers or laborers. Some of them had worked at the old mill. Most had lived in Sterling City all their lives. They hunted both bear and deer for food, in season and out. They did not value education, and they were a clan; outsiders were not welcome. I was definitely an outsider, as were most of the people who now worked at the mill, mostly as office staff.

In some ways, Sterling City reminded me of what I had read about Appalachia. Everyone in town was known in a particular way.

On Friday or Saturday nights the women in the families walked all together down Main Street to get their men out of the bar. They dragged them by their ears or other parts of their bodies. They kicked them and twisted arms. They were always successful; they got them down the street and home.

In families where everyone hunted, at least one child had been born on a hunting trip. One prominent family had a daughter named Windy. She had been born on Windy Creek. Thank God it wasn't Rattlesnake Gap. Members of this family were often leaders in the community.

CHAPTER 8

I was also like them in some ways: I had an intimate relationship with poverty. Most of my clothes were homemade or, in Oakland, bought at a thrift store or donated by the school. A staple meal was slumgullion: macaroni, onion, hamburger, and tomato sauce. When that wasn't available, we often ate bread and milk. But there were multiple ways I was not like any of them.

They were more influenced by the Southern states, while I was more influenced by rural North Dakota. The biggest difference was that I was educated. The only other educated people were the principal at the school, an occasional teacher from Paradise, a retired teacher, and the foresters. Finding teachers for the school was a real challenge.

When the *Chico Enterprise* published the story of the rape, against their policy of not publishing stories about minors, I learned about it at the local swimming pool. Adults in the community took turns sitting at the pool to supervise and watch over younger children. The day it was my turn, all the teenagers were in a huddle reading the newspaper. I suspected it could be the story of the rape, but I wanted to believe the paper had followed its policy.

It became clear it had not. All the teenagers followed me as I walked around the pool. When I stopped, they lined up and one after another dived into the water to make sure they splashed me. I watched the action and decided if they were going to continue with this behavior, they were going to look me in the eye. A teenage girl was next. I stopped and faced her and looked her directly in the eye. She dived into the pool smooth as silk—no big splash. But I knew the story was out.

Soon I learned about the petitions to get me fired as a teacher, and my husband fired from Diamond. We got threatening phone calls as did my family in Red Bluff. Everyone got letters begging them to ask us to move.

A committee of parents went to the Superintendent of Schools in Paradise requesting that I be fired. One of the women was brand new to town—she didn't know me from dirt.

The wife of the new forester, who played bridge in Red Bluff, would bring it up at every bridge game, blaming me for what happened. One of the women was a friend and told me this. I phoned the wife of the forester and suggested she stop immediately. She denied the story.

The mother of the young man told everyone in town that I told her if she gave me $7,000 I would drop the charges. I did not phone her. In that small town she was known as the town liar, but as it turned out, this time they chose to believe her. She phoned me and informed me that her husband had a weak heart and if he died of a heart attack, it would be my fault. Teenagers drove by our house yelling at me and my daughters. One woman went to every family in school who had a child in my class and offered to drive them to schools in Paradise.

In court, the judge who heard our case sent a social worker to talk to my daughter. Charlotte knew the correct name for her body parts, which led them to think she was precocious. At home, we did not refer to her vagina as her "peep-peep."

I wanted to get my daughter help. The psychologist that was recommended to us was also seeing the young man, so I found someone else. I think he was fine except he gave her an IQ test without considering how traumatized she was. We were all traumatized.

A woman in town informed me that if Frank had beaten up the young man or killed him, or if we just never said anything, it would have been all right. The town would have supported us, or at the very least believed us, and been more on our side.

Emotionally, I swung back and forth among shock, anger, and

CHAPTER 8

hurt like a yo-yo. I phoned my friend in Red Bluff almost every day. There was always some new attack.

At Halloween someone warned us that the teenagers had planned to attack our house and we needed police protection. Before Halloween arrived, in late August or early September, we decided our children were not safe attending school in Sterling City. I had an appointment for a physical in Paradise and decided to contact the priest about our three girls (Kathy now lived with us) attending the Catholic School. I made an appointment. I told him the truth about our decision and our reason for changing schools. His response was, "I will have to talk to Sister Claire Marie. We don't know what kind of influence a girl like that will have on the other girls." I was shocked and something in my body closed down. I was in profound pain for "that girl"—my daughter.

From the appointment with the priest, I went to my doctor's office for a yearly physical. I arrived in tears. The doctor did not know what to do. I could not stop crying. Should he proceed with a pelvic examination, stop and listen to me, or just stop entirely? Stopping the exam really wasn't much of an option as I worked as a teacher in Sterling City and the odds of my making the trip down the hill again soon were unlikely, if not impossible.

The Catholic school was our only real option. Anyone associated with Paradise School District probably knew the story.

Sister Claire Marie contacted me and indicated the girls could attend school. She asked the sizes of the three girls so she could order uniforms for them. A friend who worked at Safeway's meat department drove them every day to school and back home. Because he had to leave early in the morning, the girls attended Mass every school day that year.

In one of the school's festivals, Kathy was named either a

symbol of Mary or queen of something. I don't really remember. At the end of year ceremonies and at a Mass, the priest congratulated the girls for their stellar performances, having attended Mass five days a week for the entire school year. I must say, I just wanted him to shut up.

We had stayed in Sterling City almost a year and I committed to staying one more year. I made a vow. We would walk down the sidewalks of Sterling City, looking people in the eye. We would not keep it a secret because we had not done anything wrong. We protected our children, looked people in the eye, said "hello" to them. We had some support—the man who worked at Safeway and his wife, a local artist, and a few other people.

The young man was supposed to stay out of town, but every weekend he showed up. Once, Frank phoned the local sheriff's office and left a message. The sheriff stopped by our house and warned Frank about making threats. I understood whose side he was on and why.

The people of Sterling City were his people. We were not.

Chapter 9

Healing in Sterling City

Much of what had been meaningful for us about living in Sterling City was lost. Being able to walk down to the Feather River. The dog we adopted at Christmas whose pups we found homes for, and whose pups became Christmas presents. Living so close to nature. The cabin in Butte Meadows.

I knew the way I taught was alien to many of my colleagues. But I was not going to have a classroom filled with rows of desks, everyone quiet, hands folded or busily doing pages and pages out of workbooks.

My classroom was different. There was a time I convinced Red, the man who kept rattlesnakes in his refrigerator, milked them for their venom, and sold the venom, to bring a rattlesnake to school in a cage. Rattlesnakes have a unique odor and I wanted the kids in my class to recognize that odor, along with their markings, the shape of their heads, and their striking behavior.

Every hunting season, I read *Bambi* to my class—not the Walt Disney version, but the original version.

And, just as I had done in Red Bluff, I wrote a story on the blackboard about one of the kids in my class, every day a new story about a different child. I used the stories and pictures the kids drew to make a book for their parents. I asked them to draw their family. I drew a picture of each student for their book and

CHAPTER 9

wrote a story about them. Doing this helped heal the wounds for me and the town.

And then there was this: One of the women who fought hardest to get me fired asked if she could be an aide in my class. I agreed. At the end of the year, she wrote me a lovely note about what a good administrator I was and how lucky the school was to have me. I kept the card for many years.

At Christmas, I painted the front window of our home with a manger scene, put a mural of three wise men on our garage, with three or four plywood angels that I had drawn, painted and cut out. When we lived in Red Bluff I had started this tradition, plus making candles in milk cartons, pounds of candy—divinity, fudge, ganache—dozens of cookies, from Goop bars to sugar cookies, which were hung on a wooden tree, fruitcakes, zucchini and banana breads, and who knows what else. I may have started this tradition in Red Bluff, but I know I kept it going in Sterling City.

People drove up from Red Bluff, where Diamond was located, to see what I had done, and sometimes they would knock on the door. Most often they were employees of Diamond. Men brought their wives or girlfriends to meet me. Sometimes someone from Paradise or Chico would knock on the door and introduce themselves.

I was not very sophisticated; in fact, I was totally naive about men. One night we were out to dinner in Red Bluff with one of the executives at Diamond and his wife. They were a couple we spent significant time with. The man looked at me at the dinner table and said, "Come on. Let's you and I go to a motel and let these two talk."

I was dumbstruck. The evening ended and we left. I had no idea he ever gave me a second thought. He liked Frank. They were buddies. I liked his wife. They came often to Sterling City to visit. I was appalled and embarrassed.

We had a new principal at Sterling City School. His daughter was in my class. We had a pleasant enough relationship. In Sterling City people gossiped about everything and speculated about much more. One day a woman who lived across from the school shared the local gossip about me, the principal, and the supply room. I laughed and when I arrived at school, I said to him, "You will never guess what the local gossip is. The talk of the town is what good times we are having in the supply room."

With laughter, I told the story. His reply was, "If I thought I had a chance, it would not be gossip. It would be true." I believe my mouth actually dropped open. I had no idea.

When you grow up being told, "You look like Eleanor Roosevelt, the homeliest woman in the world," you looked in the mirror every day to see if it was true.

I was sure no one would want me. I think years of this teasing, combined with a mother who found fault with everything and accused me of lying on a regular basis, did enough damage to my sense of myself. I suppose another thing that did not help was my mother getting dressed up and flirting with every man who dated me.

So the gossip, or a man showing interest in me, which happened often and was totally incomprehensible to me, was very confusing.

Chapter 10

Return to Red Bluff: God at Sunday Breakfast

In Sterling City, things calmed down. My girls did well in school. I taught, and Frank had made a place for himself in the lumber industry.

Eventually the mill closed, since they had met their goal. The flume was still the only source of water. The Diamond Company, for the second time, left Sterling City. In a recent visit, I found the school building is no longer used as a school. The children are bussed to Magalia and Paradise. The town remains pretty much the same. The population has not changed much. Later I learned it was similar to many of the mountain towns tucked into the foothills and the Sierra Nevada range.

When the mill closed, we left Sterling City and the Catholic school in Paradise to return to Red Bluff. I never had to sit in Mass and listen to that priest again.

While all of this was going on, Sharon phoned from Las Vegas to announce that she would not be able to keep Kathy. When Kathy came to stay with us, I thought it was going to be temporary. But when Sharon asked if I would take her, I agreed. By that time Kathy's father, Harold, was spending time in the Sterling City bar whenever he was in town. I don't remember that he worked. He and I went to Reno to meet Kathy arriving on the bus from Las Vegas. He insisted I drive. I did not like driving, had never

CHAPTER 10

driven mountain roads, never driven a pickup. I just did not have what it took to fight with him. I just made sure I drove so badly that he decided for safety's sake and the life of his pickup, he had better drive. He was right. There wasn't much I valued. We picked up Kathy, who lived with us as our reluctant daughter until she graduated from high school. Shortly after leaving Sterling City, I wrote her dad a letter about how unhappy she was.

For whatever reason, Kathy was unhappy with the arrangement, and particularly unhappy with me. She made fun of me behind my back and complained constantly about me. I don't know why. I speculated, but to this day I am unclear about the issues for her. For me, it has always been my being told how bad I was, how wrong I was. Finally, in 2019, I gave up trying to have a civil or kind relationship with her. Of course, this is another sad story.

I taught at Bidwell School in Red Bluff where each child could set up their own curriculum and have a say regarding classroom management. Often my classrooms had the most troubled kids in the school.

It was the year the men teachers in the school decided I was out of line. They complained that I let the kids in my class come to my classroom after lunch if they chose, and they were upset that I let students use the audiovisual equipment, which they learned to use quite well.

The most troublesome boys in the school began making something like roller coasters that were designed for marble races. Watching what they learned was amazing. How to build for speed; which marbles worked best; timing the marbles; adjusting the clay-built tracks to increase speed. I learned that given support, they would find a way to learn.

I remember a boy who had been told, "If you would only settle down and study, you would do fine." I told him it was his choice to find his own way to learn, which he did.

I had a girl in the class sitting at her desk crying. I walked back to talk to her and this is the conversation (my class graded their own papers):

"What's the matter, Suzie?"

"I'm used to getting all A's."

"Well, give yourself all A's."

"I know I don't deserve them."

While I was teaching, other teachers were meeting with the principal to get rid of me. The expectation was that my classes would do so poorly in achievement tests provided by the state, that the principal would have cause to fire me. They did not do poorly and I could not be fired.

BACK TO RED BLUFF

When we left Sterling City, we looked for land to build yet another house, living in a motel while we looked. All six of us shared just two rooms. Of course, Tony, our son, set fire to the grass next to the foundation of the motel, so we had to find a house to rent. We rented a house in the subdivision where my brother lived in Red Bluff.

We found twenty acres off of Baker Road outside of town to

CHAPTER 10

build our home. I always hoped for a view and sunset. It was not to be.

I loved driving down Main Street toward Redding and seeing Mount Shasta, a mountain filled with myths, spirits, religion and much more. I loved that mountain. I talked to it as I had talked to the tall pine trees in Sterling City. As a child, I talked to myself, the air, the road ... .

Jack Mulligan, who built our first house in Red Bluff, built the new house. We sold all but seven acres. The new house had more of the features I wanted. A pantry, not a walk-in pantry but an oversized cupboard called a pantry. Our family room was an extension of the kitchen, the place we spent most of our time. A fireplace that was open to both the family room and the living room kept us warm all winter.

There was a large living room and formal dining room, an entryway with a hall that led to the bedrooms. The master bedroom had a huge closet which was good since I had an extensive wardrobe provided by a friend in Sterling City who had had breast reduction surgery.

Besides the master bedroom there were three others. Char and Beth shared one large bedroom. Their biggest disagreement was that Beth was neat and her sister was not. Kathy had her own room as did Tony. Kathy's room was the neatest. Tony's was the messiest.

It was my children's favorite house. I loved it and I am sure Frank did also.

My parents had come back from Utah, and we put a mobile home in the back for them. They had tried to live in Utah where my brother and his family lived, but it had not worked out well.

As my parents settled into the mobile home, my dad and Frank put in a huge garden. They worked on it every evening after work. Frank's nickname for my dad was "Slick." They loved each other. I think my dad was the father Frank never had. It was a pleasure to see them together. Their gardening deeply influenced Charlotte, who now has her own garden.

I continued working. I was teaching at Bidwell School. I usually brought the girls home, but one time I forgot Beth. It was not an unusual thing to happen. I knew this as a teacher waiting for a parent to arrive, but being both a teacher and a parent who forgot her child, well, I was deeply ashamed and embarrassed.

Bidwell was not a good fit for me, so I was moved to junior high where I taught sixth grade. The principals there were at a loss as to what to do with me, especially since the three superintendents of school thought I was exceptional. I read everything I could about teaching from works about the English primary school Summerhill. I read all the child development books I could find and all the parenting books. I took a parenting class. I knew two things: I wanted to be a different parent than the ones I had, and I wanted to teach children in a way that could deepen their love of learning. I worked hard at being a different kind of mother and teacher than I saw around me.

Before we left Sterling City, I applied to participate in a summer program designed for teachers who worked with disadvantaged youth in Chico. Initially, I was not chosen to be a participant. I am not sure it occurred to anyone how disadvantaged many of our rural areas were. I often think of them as the most neglected areas in our country. I was desperate. I pleaded. I begged, and, finally, I was accepted.

I think I was the only person there from a rural area. I was assigned to the preschool/kindergarten age. There was a little boy who got off the bus and immediately came looking for me calling, "Where's the White teacher?" until he found me. The staff all laughed because one of the other teachers was even more

CHAPTER 10

blond and light-skinned than I was.

We had one gifted little girl, the last of ten children. All her siblings suffered from mental limitations. We hoped we could provide her with stimulation unavailable in the home.

A nun on the staff joined a group of us teachers in the cafeteria in a conversation about Black children. When she announced that Blacks smell, there was an uproar at the table. I thought it was a good thing no one from the staff was there.

Of course, I had my own faux pas. A Black woman on the staff was competent, dedicated, fierce, and a powerful force. We were standing outside the building chatting and she joined us. I said "hello" and commented on her dress. "I like your dress. You look good in white." A pause as she looked at me and then thanked me. Ouch! I was guilty and I knew it. Her look said it all. I thought long and hard about how to rectify my behavior. I waited three days and when we gathered together again, she looked at me and said, "You look good in black." I thanked her and added, "I like it also." We were even. The incident never came up again. What changed was the energy in the room.

During that program we visited housing for farmworkers. Some were adequate and some were so minimal that you wondered how people got up in the morning to work: six people in one room, walking half a block to a bathroom with running water. I have never had the courage to take on all the injustices I witnessed.

My early reputation in Red Bluff as a "loose woman" had finally gone to the graveyard to rest. One last reminder did occur one evening when Frank and I went separately to a gathering at the Chicken Shack. As Frank told me the story, the man next to him, looking at me, said, "Here comes the only woman who can be fully dressed and look naked." Frank looked at him and said,

"That's my wife." The man, whom I knew, made a speedy exit. These kinds of situations still made me scared, overly cautious. I was tired of being seen as some kind of sex symbol or other, less attractive labels. It changed something in me that made me want to be invisible. I tried often to be invisible.

At home, our lives were organized. Everyone in the house, except Tony (too young) and Frank, cooked. We took turns. The girls each cooked one meal a week, always dinner. For other meals, everyone was on their own. Beth cooked on Wednesdays. Every Wednesday, and I mean *every* Wednesday, we had hot dogs with macaroni and cheese. If I hadn't insisted on a vegetable after about two months of macaroni and cheese and hot dogs, we might have eaten that every Wednesday for a long, long time.

One night Charlotte put a bowl of spaghetti on the table—no sauce, just a bowl of spaghetti. Again, I protested, "This is not an adequate meal." I gave everyone a description of an adequate meal and the expectations I had. Though that night we ate the plain spaghetti.

Kathy cooked her meal-a-week and did a good job.

Once a week we made a housecleaning list. Everyone was responsible for their own bedroom. Charlotte and Beth, who shared a room, had conflict over who was the messiest. Charlotte won that prize. Beth drew a line down the middle of the room, letting her sister know she was to stay on her side and never cross the line.

My son's bedroom would eventually become such a mess, piled high with junk, dirty dishes, apple cores, and dirty clothes that the room had to be emptied in order to clean it.

Everyone got an allowance, and a raise on their birthdays, no strings attached. On weekends everyone chose a room to clean besides their bedroom. Dining room, kitchen, family room,

CHAPTER 10

living room and bathroom. They rotated through the house. I always cleaned the bathroom the following Saturday when it was my son's turn to clean. I was teaching. For me, this plan served two purposes: 1) they learned necessary skills that would serve them when they left home and, 2) they learned to cooperate for the benefit of family. One thing that surprised me was how rarely they fought, how they worked things out. Kathy may have been the only exception. She continued to be unhappy and I felt she believed I was responsible for her unhappiness. In retrospect, it seems understandable.

Sunday breakfast was a must. Either Frank or I cooked. We ate at the dining table and often breakfast lasted two or three hours. It was one of my favorite times.

When we first moved into our new home, five-year-old Tony announced, "I talked to God today."

"What did God look like?" I responded, totally forgetting what was important. When I recognized it was the wrong question, I asked, "What did God say?"

"He said this isn't a very good place. People don't have time for each other." I decided we could fix that. It was out of that conversation that Sunday morning breakfast became a tradition and an effort was made to improve the situation. Maybe a week or two later my son came into the kitchen and again announced, "I talked to God today."

"What did God say?" I asked.

"God said, 'This is a good place. The people here have time for each other.'"

Chapter 11

1957: Sputnik and Special Ed in Red Bluff

When summer arrived, I took classes at Chico State. I enjoyed classes on teaching and exploring the social and psychological implications of public school education.

Sometime during these years, Russia launched Sputnik. The competitiveness between the two countries was a lot like a sixth grader puffing up, like swagger.

Because the country was now competing in the space race, schools were rewriting curricula to emphasize science and math. In my mind, when art was gone and then music, followed by social studies and health, what was left was only math, science, reading, and history, all taught from books. Exploration, problem-solving, experimenting, and working together were gone. It was like a death-blow.

Another influential event in my life in those years was the decision to start a new special education class for neurologically handicapped children. Glen Smith, the superintendent, talked to me and made arrangements for me to visit his wife's class in Antelope School. It was unlike any classroom I had ever visited.

I thought I might try it, so certain agreed-upon children were recommended by teachers. The school psychologist tested them to be sure they qualified. The class was almost always made up of boys, with an occasional girl. Their behavior was intense, some-

CHAPTER 11

times violent, often self-attacking, and rarely calm. The first class was all boys of various ages between six and twelve years old, loud and boisterous. Getting to know them and what the issues were that interfered with their learning and ability to manage themselves, I soon discovered the value of animals. We always had a white rat in the class, living in a glass cage.

One little boy about eight years old would head for the cage first thing in the morning, get the rat out, and put it on his shoulder. There it stayed almost every day for an hour or more, until a new activity caught the boy's attention; he was a boy who just couldn't sit still. Before the rat, he had been a regular classroom disturbance. In my classroom two things kept him quiet and cooperative. One was the white rat and the other was any hands-on activity, such as building—or figuring out how to build—something.

There was a first grader who had an unusual relationship with other creatures. He would hold a bee in his hand, go around the room and show it off to the other students. He never got stung.

One time the class visited his house, which was on a cattle ranch. He was sitting on a hill and as I walked toward him up the hill, I asked, "What are you doing?"

"Killing a rattlesnake."

His father, close by, came moving fast, and in front of the boy, less than three inches away from him, was a dead rattlesnake.

I let the students make up their own spelling lists. Their favorite spelling words were swear words, from "fuck" to "bastard," and a long list of similar words. "Shit" was one of their favorites.

After writing down the list of words they had given me, I would give it to them and tell them when they had learned how to spell a word, let me know. Or they could take them home and study them until they knew them. Pretty soon some boy would yell, "Mrs. Ghio, I know how to spell 'motherfucker.'" He would spell the word correctly, and I would take it off his list. Then I would choose a word for him. Sometimes they never did learn the word I gave them.

I had a workbench in my classroom. I also had chisels, saws and hammers. They could learn to make a wooden tray or bowl. They made bookcases with many flaws and with great pride. Everyone made something except the youngest, and perhaps the boy who loved the rat.

One boy was very abused. He was not angry at his abusive father, but furious with his mother for letting it happen and not protecting him.

One boy set his house on fire. The police contacted me, as the boy indicated he would only talk to me. He told me he had started the fire and walked as slowly as he could to the neighbors. His family members were very troubled, and very good Christians.

I suppose the boy who still most lives in my heart is the boy with all the flapping and other symptoms of a neurological problem. He had an older brother. His mother seemed to hate both him and me, which I could understand. They left as a family for South Africa, where their father planned to practice medicine. He was a general practitioner in Red Bluff. In fact, he was my doctor, and the one whom I consulted when a boy came to school with a highly contagious disease.

I never saw any of them again. The story I heard was that the father, the doctor, collapsed in the train depot and died of a heart attack. Some years later, I heard that my student, who was a young adult by that time, had killed his mother, had shot her nineteen times. The story touches my own grief and sadness.

CHAPTER 11

And then, one day after a vacation, I came in to teach only to discover that my classroom had been packed up and moved to another school!

I have many things from those years to regret. I was teaching a brand-new program that no one knew anything about. The teacher in Antelope was helpful but it wasn't enough. It never occurred to me to ask for help or support. One of the school psychologists did support me, but she had a full-time caseload. The other teacher complained about how much information I put in my reports. The stress was overwhelming.

I still carry a deep regret for how I treated one boy's parents, both high school PE teachers. They had taken into their home two boys that they hoped to adopt. One was in my classroom. One day I said to him, "I don't know what I am going to do with you," in a light manner, and he said to me, "Yes, you do, Mrs. Ghio. You know I am going to be okay."

His adopted parents worried, and their fear was making him more insecure. Their demands were not helpful. I wrote them a letter of more than one page, naming all their sins. To this day I feel badly about that letter. It was unkind, arrogant, and not at all helpful. It was a terrible thing to do.

Chapter 12

Everything Changes Once Again

The minister at the church attended by the family whose son had walked slowly from the burning house came to me as a friend. He arrived at school before Christmas and begged me to quit or take a break. I was a mess, but asking for help was not an option. By the time I was five I had learned from my mother that help was not available. She did not allow it for any of us, nor could she ask for or accept help for herself.

I was deteriorating rapidly. I was deeply depressed. I began actively to plan how to kill myself. I wanted to be sure it looked like an accident. A friend of mine was speeding across a train track and was hit. Her death was declared an accident. I knew better.

At first, I was just thinking of an accidental death. I then began to plan in actuality. I had to cross railroad tracks on one of the ways I drove home. I began to drive that way, planning how to have a train hit me, to learn when the trains crossed the intersection, get to know the exact times, know how to make it look like my car had stalled or how to be assured my car arrived minutes before the train. I went on with my daily routine. One day driving to work, my chest hurt so badly I decided I didn't have to commit suicide. If I just continued like I was, I would be dead within the year, so I quit planning how to kill myself. I went through the motions of being alive.

CHAPTER 12

The '60s were the time of psychotherapeutic marathons—three or four days of no sleep, little food, and a lot of processing. A friend of mine had attended one and came home singing its praises. I decided to attend one. My friend raved about the leader of the one he attended. I made arrangements, drove to Chico, found the location. The leader was a teacher at Chico State. The room was filled with twenty-year-olds. Not long after it started, I wondered what in the hell I was doing there. One college student was crying because she was still a virgin and so embarrassed that she kept it a secret. Times had definitely changed. Someone accused me of being "the mothering type," which was probably true, since I assumed that role early in my life, much to my brothers' dismay. Early on, during the weekend, I began crying and couldn't stop. I cried continuously for three days. The students tried to take care of me. The leader was beside himself. When I finally stopped crying, I drove home a new person. I had found a courage that was new to me.

The first thing I did when I arrived home was to throw out the half-empty jar of amphetamines I had used to lose weight. They came from the Oakland drugstore in a quart plastic container; at one time it was full. I had spent most of my life attempting to improve myself, fix myself, be acceptable, so that maybe then I would be loved.

The second thing I did was announce I wanted a divorce. I find this particularly sad. Frank was a good man. On occasion, alcohol would become a problem, but it was short-lived. He was full-blooded Italian. He was a simple man, practical. He worked hard, came home, sat in his favorite chair, drank a beer and watched his children. I did not have any plans for a divorce prior to that weekend. Occasionally, it would cross my mind; I had never taken it seriously.

I would joke with him about my sister-in-law. "You never will have to worry about having someone. She will be right here."

Which proved to be true. My children and I had a field day figuring out the relationship of aunt to stepmother, and so on. Cousins to stepbrothers and stepsisters.

Frank moved out of the house and I continued to teach for a while, and then I decided to go to graduate school at Chico State. I quit teaching and commuted to Chico for at least a semester. Then the house sold and the kids and I moved there. We had twenty-seven cats prior to this. We also had an owl who was injured, a crow at one time, and an assortment of guinea pigs and white rats. We also had a dog who had come with us from Sterling City.

I loaned my washer and dryer and some furniture to friends. These things were destroyed when they had a house fire.

We found a duplex in Chico and moved into it. It was the only time I remember one of my children getting sick. Beth had a fever and in general felt horrible.

During this time, I hired an attorney. Frank and I used the same one; we had no disagreement. We went to court together and sat together. The judge, who I believe was on his third marriage, began by questioning us about why we were getting a divorce. His first comment was, "I don't understand how you can come to court together and can't stay married."

Then the judge was unhappy with our child support agreement and called me up to the stand questioning me about why I wasn't asking for more money. I was asking for $150 a month.

After the divorce, my sister-in-law pursued Frank and my brother—her husband—caught them in bed. It got out of control, and my brother ended up in jail. I think my mother blamed me. According to her, there would have not been a problem if I had behaved properly. She asked me if I would bail my brother out of jail. I said no.

CHAPTER 12

The attorney who handled our divorce congratulated us and announced all divorces should be so amicable. Over the years we remained friendly.

Frank continued to see my sister-in-law. Eventually they got married. When he had filed for divorce but never picked up the papers, they reconnected and went to Fall River. It was a time when not much was stable. Frank returned to Red Bluff alone, finally picking up the divorce papers, then left Red Bluff and never returned. His leaving was a deep loss for my father and for Frank, also.

While living in the Red Bluff house, I had a few parties. A new friend from Chico, Linnet, came, and a few other people.

We didn't live in the duplex long before Linnet suggested we live together, which we did. She had three children and I had three. Charlotte had a bedroom of her own. Tony and her youngest child, a boy, shared a room. Beth and her middle child, also a girl, shared a room. Both were named Elizabeth. They tolerated each other. My daughter announced a few years later, "If I could get along with Beth L., I can get along with anyone." From her life and career, I would say that this was true.

Their mother was a student also. She was smart, sexy and seductive. She always had a new man to share her bed. On the campus, faculty members and foreign students found her appealing. She was a party girl.

At Chico State, I went to graduate school with a major in counseling psychology. I planned to get both my counseling and school psychologist's license, which I did.

While Linnet and I lived together, Char and Linnet's son Paul would plant marijuana in gallon milk cartons and hide them under the oak tree across the street. Donald and Tony would, with great determination, march across the street and carry them home announcing they were going to be narcs when they grew up.

We lived in an old two-story house on Dayton Road in Chico. My dad helped do some repairs in the attic so Paul could have a bedroom. Dad was an amazing carpenter: skilled, efficient and knowledgeable. I watched him repair a window—hanging on, leaning out the window—while I stood in terror.

The rooms had numbers on the doors.

"What is this, a whorehouse?" my dad asked me one day.

"Why, no, why do you ask?"

"Numbers on the upstairs bedroom doors."

Well, here I was, living in a whorehouse. I was embarrassed and shocked. Not too much later, I learned it was also a drug house, a pot house. A place you could buy a variety of drugs, from marijuana to LSD. My roommate was more into drugs than I was. We had one party that lasted three days. My roommate loved it. Even though Dayton Road was a wild ride for me, I was in awe!

During that time, Char moved out of her room and began sleeping on the back porch. I don't remember why. It may have been that we needed help, and so my roommate decided we needed another roommate, a man capable of doing repairs. We interviewed a few. One I still know.

While Char was sleeping on the back porch, she somehow found a cage and caught a mouse. The caged mouse lived on the back porch with her and at night the other mice would come visit and talk to the captive one. It would keep Char awake. Then one particularly hot day, the mouse died. The whole house was sad.

CHAPTER 12

Chico and Red Bluff were as different as could be. No one gossiped about me in Chico. There was nothing to gossip about. There was much more individual freedom. The rules were no longer hard and fast, they changed from place to place and were often forgotten altogether. Red Bluff social rules were much more set in stone. Of course, that was not going to last. Things began to loosen up everywhere, even in rural America. A new set of morals was developing, changing the world as we knew it, almost faster than I could breathe.

I was now an intern at the counseling center. We were supervised by the staff. At one point I was assigned to the nursing department where young soon-to-be-nurses were learning to give shots. They practiced on me.

I was also eventually assigned to the Day Care Center, which was run by a group of "hippies" who often came to work stoned and rarely interacted with the children. I got the message to clean the place up. The other person who applied for the job was part of the in-group. She didn't get it and her followers began to act out. I had to fire some. Not a task I had any experience with and one I was not skilled in. I took a class in child development and knew if I stayed at Chico, I could get a job teaching in the Child Development program.

My children seemed to be doing well. Tony had a buddy. Once they got in trouble and the police brought them home. Beth kept to herself and avoided things she did not like or approve of. Char and Paul were fast friends. Char used marijuana with Paul. One night, she tried something else, then sat on a dining room chair and pulled down her pants and urinated. I asked what she was on and she swore it was vodka. Whatever it was, it cured her of her idealization of a drugged/drinking experience.

We lived on a roller coaster. Four actual teenagers, two eight-year-olds and, as a couple of counselors at the counseling center pointed out to me, one mother—me—and one perpetual teenager.

One day Linnet announced she was moving to Alaska. At that point I was neither surprised nor disappointed. I was relieved.

We gave notice. She packed up her things. We had a yard sale and she asked me to keep some chairs for her and a table. I still have the chairs after several moves of my own. The table recently left my home. She packed up her car, hooked up a trailer, piled in her children, and headed for Ketchican, Alaska.

I moved into a house that was reputed to be the oldest house in Chico, part of the original Valencia Ranch. It could certainly have been true—it was a very old house with a long porch around the living room all the way to the kitchen. On the porch was an old-fashioned wringer washing machine, which I continued to use. Before I came to Chico I made clothes to last me until I graduated. I was on a very tight budget.

I volunteered at the Crisis Center and there I met Doug Baer, who was going to play a big role in my life. Two people served as aides in my Educational Handicap Class in Red Bluff. The other, my ex-babysitter, was majoring in education at Chico State. She was now a friend, and very good at her job.

The Child Care Center had been taken over by the student body. Ruth Swanson, the director of the Child Development lab, was gone. The Child Care Center and then-nursery was in an-

CHAPTER 12

other building. I volunteered at the Child Care Center and when the job for director became available, I had just completed my masters and had no plans. I was asked if I was interested. I said yes and applied for the job.

The staff was made up of the counterculture, who gave little direction and often seemed to just want to be there and keep a distance from the children. In some way, I agreed with them. From my viewpoint, our children had been over-directed, manipulated and controlled.

The woman who was in charge of the nursery worked under my direction. Our budget was quite tight—in many ways too tight. She asked for money that was not there. She was usually asking for money to provide the snacks. I suggested she ask parents to help. Her response was angry and demanding, since she felt parents should not have to help because many of them were so poor. The truth was we were all poor. They were students. I was newly graduated.

One of the things I did was make a long, bright pink dress with the children's handprints on it. I wore it to school. I wore it to "The Bridge," the crisis center where I worked. I led a group, answered the phone, and greeted drop-ins.

A drop-in joined the group I was leading one night, troubled, lost and tired. He started talking, crying, despondent and depressed. I just let him talk as he managed to tear a chair apart while he talked and cried. I watched. Finally, he took a breath and, in shock, looked at the chair. The legs were pulled away from the seat as was the back of the chair. The seat lay on the floor. He looked at me with dark fear.

"Why don't you take the chair pieces and move them out of your way?" He looked at me in terror, but when nothing horrible happened, he began to cry again, and for a very long time. We all waited. He came to himself, stopped crying, looked around the room and settled into himself. He came back every week until I left.

One day I was in the Crisis Center. Doug had returned from Easter some time in the past couple of weeks. A new woman that he had met was also expected to arrive. He was excited. She had three children.

She introduced herself to me on a day I was wearing my long, pink dress covered with handprints. To this day, over forty years later, I consider her one of the dearest women I have ever known. I love Karen and her husband, Doug, dearly.

Years later, they led me to Nevada City. And thereby hangs yet another tale!

Chapter 13

Full Circle

She sat in the car, her mouth tight, twitching, sometimes speaking to herself.

"I wish I never had her or any of them. Why did I marry him? Four kids later and here I sit stewing in the car. I should have run away when I finished high school. I could have gone to Chicago—gotten a job and gone to art school or become a writer. Chicago, now, in early spring. No, I don't think so. Maybe New York. Yes, I want to be in New York living in a penthouse apartment with a cleaning lady and a cook. If I never clean another toilet, mop another floor, ever see her again or cook another pound of hamburger to feed six people, I would be happy and content. What happened to me? My life is a shambles. Oh, here she comes."

"Hi Mom. How are you doing?"

"I think we should never see each other."

"Oh? How did you decide that?"

"Our relationship is too hard on you."

"You're right. It is a hard relationship and I'll stop seeing you if that is what you want. It is not what I want."

"Just take me home."

CHAPTER 13

The silence was anything but quiet. The air was filled with old hurts, anger, despair, pain, sorrow. I stopped the car.

"Just let me out. Don't come in."

"I am coming in. We are going to talk, the two of us."

"Why do you always want to talk?" she screams. "Can't you ever leave well enough alone? No one wants to talk about all this stuff. Your brothers dread seeing you come for a visit. No one knows what you will dig up next. Can't you just be quiet? Shut up for a change!"

I was stunned. She's right! No one in this family wants to talk about all this stuff.

"Well, if you want anything, I'll be downstairs."

The nurse came and checked her.

The social worker came. My mother told her about North Dakota, her adored father, her evil mother and mean sisters.

The minister called. "Can I come today?"

"I'll check."

"No, I don't want to see him." The day before she had agreed. "I wish he would quit calling."

The social worker said, "What an interesting, bright woman she is. Imagine! Eight kids in one bedroom."

I heard her admiration and wanted to tell her the truth, but I didn't.

Sophia, an assistant, helped prepare me.

"She won't come downstairs."

"She had to do this her way, Ruth."

"She won't use the oxygen, all she eats and drinks is Kentucky

Fried Chicken, Jello, chocolate pudding and Jim Beam."

"You both are letting go," Sophia assured me.

Every day when she made it harder and harder, I reminded myself "She has to do this her way," I wondered why I had thought this time would be different.

I bought her Barbara Bush's autobiography. I knew she was sick when she quit reading. The TV blared on and on, always news and politics.

She fell out of bed one night. She lay there until I heard her call, "Ralph! Ralph!" I jumped out of bed and managed to get her settled again.

Now every night I checked on her two, three times and I listened. Often she called for my father.

One night when she got up to go to the bathroom, I couldn't help her.

The rescue team came, got her into bed and gave me a number to call next time.

"She has to do this her way," I reminded myself.

There were conversations with my brothers.

"How's she doing?"

"She wants to go to a nursing home."

"Again?!"

"Well, you know Mom."

"Is she eating?"

"Usually. Last night she fell. I barely got her back into bed."

"Is she hurt?"

CHAPTER 13

"No. She won't use a hospital bed. The doctor says she should get out, but she won't leave the house."

"Man, she can be stubborn."

"Tell me about it, but she has to do this her way," I say aloud to remind myself.

"Let me talk to her."

"Okay ..."

"Mom, it's Franklin."

Every day I either phoned them or they phoned me. Our conversations were always about her. Franklin remembering out loud.

"Boy she loves the Democrats. We had some good discussions."

"I'm going to miss the battle of opinions."

In my family I always lost those battles. I wouldn't miss them.

The next day it would be Irvin. The conversation was mostly the same.

"Remember the time I was going to buy a house in Sacramento and she kept talking about the HUD scandal? When I asked what that had to do with my buying a house, she answered. "I don't know. Something."

"Sounds like her. Is she still hot about Evelyn and Cal?"

"I avoid the topic."

"She sure holds a grudge."

"Yeah, it took her nine years and my confronting her to get her to quit blaming me for her being hospitalized."

"I don't remember that. Can she talk?"

"I think so. Mom, it's Irvin."

Soon she quit eating. "Nothing appeals to me."

Then she couldn't get up. Chris and I changed her, helped keep her clean. The aide taught us how to change the bedding. We cut her nightgown up the back to make it easier.

She got thinner. She didn't eat. I gave her a little water. They gave me swabs to use. She might drown. Three or four times a night she would slide almost out of bed. I would put her back.

She became cooler, clammy, and she no longer needed changing.

My brothers called. Finally Irv and June came to visit.

Irv walked into the house, took one look at her and bolted. In the pickup was a case of beer. He sat on the deck for fifteen minutes drinking. He had had enough. They left.

Thanksgiving Day she lay upstairs.

Laura, my niece, tended to her. She was training to be a nurse. Kevin, Ralph's son, came. He couldn't go upstairs to see her.

I checked on her with Laura.

She didn't speak. She lay there with tears seeping out of her eyes and a look of fear and sometimes sorrow.

Her look was haunting to me. I've never described it well. There is no way to describe it. She never closed her eyes.

I tried to close them but I'd check again and they were open.

When my brothers phoned, we held the phone to her ear—no response.

My grandkids played downstairs—tiptoed up once to visit her.

We ate dinner; talked, laughed and drank.

On Saturday, her breathing changed. We took off the oxygen

CHAPTER 13

we had put on weeks before. Laura checked her breathing.

"It's all right, Grandma. Can you hear me?"

Laura rubbed her feet. I came upstairs. "She's going."

I went upstairs just in time to watch her die.

Everyone had gone home except Laura, John, Kevin and my friend Stephanie.

We talked, phoned family, my brothers, sat with her and then called them to come and get her.

"Why don't you wait in another part of the house?"

"No," I responded.

Kevin went into another room crying.

We watched them take her out on the gurney in a brown body bag.

I walked into the empty room still aware of her presence and of her face. The look still haunts me. I won't forget it for a long time.

We made arrangements to have her cremated. Unlike my father, there were no final wishes. "You decide—I don't care." She had few, if any, friends.

We held the service in a Mormon church in Red Bluff. The church, I think, that she blamed for stealing her favorite son from her.

My niece played the piano. Tim's wife sang and my brother Franklin officiated. I spoke. Her youngest brother did not come. He was facing his own death and would follow her in exactly one month.

Beth, my daughter, did not come. My father's death was enough for her.

At my brother's house, again we gathered.

We had said goodbye in the ways we knew.

I didn't cry. I was too unsure about how I felt.

I was relieved to have this difficult relationship end. I wondered what my brothers and I would talk about.

Three months later, I carried her ashes to Red Bluff. My brother Irv ordered the headstone for both of them.

Over 60 years they had fought, complained, separated, reunited, over and over again.

Now they lie together in the same place as my brother. In the place he had loved, and she had hated. So it goes as in life it is in death.

I hated her for a while. I felt haunted by her criticism, her judgment. She would not go away. She still comes looking at me with recrimination. I don't hate her. I don't love her. I miss her. She was a complex, brilliant, tormented woman. My deepest grief for her is her unlived life. Last year, I dedicated an altar to her, and to all women like her:

> *"To all the women who, because of fear, demands of marriage, and the culture, did not live their intelligence or creativity. They are a loss to all of us. In her torment she hurt us all."*

I miss her, I wanted to love her, be loving to her. Was I? I don't think so. It was too hard. I wanted her to love me first.

Imagination Running Wild ...

... short fiction

Red
September 9, 2012

Her face was swollen, black and blue. There was a cut on her chin where his ring had hit her jaw. One eye was swollen shut. Her black hair, carefully coiffed earlier, was now straggly and matted with blood.

The room was shabby. The couch was uneven, covered with an old, worn, Indian spread. The chair that had once matched the couch had springs hanging out. The floor was a drab gray and in the center was a piece of linoleum decorated with violent red roses. Sitting on the linoleum was a kitchen table littered with leftover food from Carl's Jr.: old fries and dried ketchup. Beer cans that had been used for ashtrays lay on the table, spilling out wet cigarette butts, tobacco, beer and ashes. On each side of the table were two chairs. They were old, with broken backs and rickety legs. The peeling paint on the table and chairs was an old putrid green.

Like everything in the house, the table and chairs had a grimy quality. It had been a long time since they had been cleaned. On one wall were a door and two windows which led to a dilapidated porch and a cracked sidewalk. Weeds grew everywhere—through the cracks of the porch floorboards, and up through the cracks in the sidewalk. Outside, on the sidewalk, was the door to the "john" as he called it, and a door to the one bedroom. Across the back wall were a stove, sink, and refrigerator set into a dingy metal cupboard. The bedroom next to the bathroom was dark, cluttered with clothes strung everywhere. The room smelled of sweat, musky and sweet. He had gone to get more beer. "To cool off," he said.

She looked at her red high-heeled shoes as tall as stilts. They made her legs long and shapely. The back of her red dress was split just barely to her ass; her black nylons were now in shreds.

He had teasingly asked if she wore red panties too. He could see her red bra when she leaned over to pick up her beer can or light another cigarette from the match he offered. She often leaned forward to entice him, just a little.

She went to the bathroom and looked into the broken mirror. Tears rolled down her face from swollen eyes, over the bruises and down her neck. She touched her face gently, noticed the bruises on her arms, especially the one on her wrist where he had grabbed her and twisted it until she screamed in pain. Finally, she gently washed her face. Found her purse and the comb. Carefully she combed out the tangles and then leaned over into the metal shower stall to rinse the blood out of her hair. She combed it and braided it.

She found her torn black nylons, her red panties, and then carefully removed her bra, slipping the shoulders of her dress down, unsnapping it and wriggling until it fell to the floor. She cleaned up the table with a sponge, sweeping everything into a paper bag. She picked up the miscellaneous trash. Did the dishes and put them into the cupboard. She washed down the table. She did not hurry. She knew about how much time she had. She took the bag of trash out the door and set it at the side of the house. She gathered up her nylons, bra and panties and put them in a metal bowl in the sink.

She took the matches down from above the stove and carefully lit the items in the bowl, watching as they ignited into flames and burned until there was nothing left but the straps of her bra and a small pile of ashes. She opened the door and, holding the bowl with a towel, she threw the ashes to the wind. Then she went into the bedroom and opened the closet door. The 12-gauge shotgun was where she expected to find it.

He had bragged, "Ain't nobody ever going to bother me, nobody going to hurt me. See this baby, well she ain't ever empty. I keep it loaded all the time just in case. Never even put the safety on, 'cause you gotta be damn fast."

She didn't even bother to check the gun; she knew it was loaded. She took it out and laid it on the table. She found an old saucer for an ashtray. Went to her purse where she found a pack of cigarettes. She moved the chair so it was facing the door. She looked at the clock and reckoned she had about five or ten minutes. She lit a cigarette, sat in the old rickety chair facing the door, picked up the shotgun, steadied it on the table with her finger on the trigger, and watched and waited.

Child of Goodness

She hid behind the door and watched. The look was of pure glee! Bam! She kicked me! She runs, laughing. I collect myself.

"I'll get even," I think quietly to myself and I am shocked at the thought. After all I am the adult. Yet, I cannot help myself as I wait and watch for a time to get her. Because somehow the adult had disappeared and I am a child again, indulging in a childish power struggle.

I washed the dishes, humming off key. I swept the floor, glancing over my shoulder. I knew she would get hungry. I fiddled around in the kitchen. A child walked in with a look of innocence.

I believe in goodness and was crushed. How could I think? How could I plan such a thing? I was at the sink as she approached. I threw the icy cold water squarely in her face. She howled and went looking righteously for someone to report my meanness to. I stood smiling smugly. I didn't believe in meanness and yet I was mean. I felt even more smug but under the smugness a deep humiliation. I hated myself and I hated her for making me hate myself.

I waited for someone to confront me, even though I know I'm too old for scolding. No one came. My smugness began to weaken a little. I didn't need it any longer. It is gone but what is left? An awareness, a kind of a sickening awareness. I sat down at the kitchen table, ashamed and defeated.

I heard a scurrying noise. I listened carefully. What did it mean? Was it a noise of danger or was it friendly? I looked around frantically. I couldn't discern if it was friendly or dangerous. I listened intently. I still heard the scurrying noise. Then silence, black inky silence. I listened carefully. Still silence. I could not bear it. I pushed my chair back cautiously, not even a squeak. I lifted my body up. I heard my knees creak. I stopped, almost holding my breath. I stole across the living room. Slithered towards the hall. And then I screamed and screamed!

Again that same damn laughter.

"I don't believe in meanness," through gritted teeth. "I don't believe in meanness," with each in-breath. "I don't believe in meanness," with each straightening of each vertebra.

Calmly, I walk down the hall, knowing she is trapped in either the bathroom or one of the three bedrooms. I leave the dead snake lying there. She will pick it up, I promise myself. I check the bathroom—the shower, under the sink, and behind the door. I close the door and lock it. Next, a bedroom, under the bed. I use a stick to poke into the closet, behind the drapes, under the dresser. The last place to look, behind the door. I close that door. Two rooms left. One straight ahead, one to my left. If I go straight ahead she could sneak past me. No matter what I do, she can escape me.

I stopped and waited and listened. I stood very still and listened for about fifteen minutes. "I don't believe in meanness," a voice sings in my head. Finally a noise. It was not a big noise, just sort of a sniffle. I reminded myself as I smiled, "I don't believe in meanness." I was caught in this primitive place and I was out of control and I was scared, but I proceeded.

I walk into the end room. There she is. A child of goodness, smiling, friendly. I believe in goodness, but I can't find any in myself at that moment. I walk towards her. I smile back. She watches me. She is leery. I move closer. I grab her by the arm, by her hair and drag her as she yells for help. I drag her to the dead snake. I order her to pick it up. She is scared and I am delighted.

"Pick it up," I scream. I push her face down towards the snake. She picks it up. I release my grip slightly. Damn! She escapes and throws the snake in my direction. I feel it wrap around me as it hits my hips. I am repulsed. I crash onto the sofa, too tired to go any further.

Exhausted and defeated, I sit. I feel the taste of meanness in my chest. I ask myself, "What happened? Who was I? How did I ... ?" I couldn't finish the question. I was rising out of a deep fog. I was stunned. I don't believe in meanness and yet I am mean, very mean. I sit with the sense of meanness. It has seeped into every part of me now. No cell is free from this shameful sense of meanness.

I don't know how long I sat. The room darkened and I sat quiet, reflecting sadly on my meanness and myself. Because I don't believe in meanness doesn't mean I am not capable of being mean or hateful. "What pushes me into it? Whose fault is it? If I don't believe in being mean, how do I do it? How am I so mean?"

As I am lost in my thoughts, a tear-stained face appears in the kitchen doorway. I don't see the stained face in the darkness, I just know it. I hear the bare footsteps moving slowly closer. I see her goodness. I believe in this child of goodness. She stands quietly in front of me. "Sorry," she says.

I believe in this child of goodness. I don't believe in meanness, yet I am mean. Quietly together we sit. I hold her, absently, I stroke her hair. She lays her head on my lap and I continue to stroke her hair, her face, and I massage her tiny body. The tears began to stream down my face, and my body is racked with sobs that I hold inside, tightly.

As I look down on her, filled with remorse and regret, my mind—or perhaps it is my soul—goes to another long-ago child cowering in the corner, filled with terror, fending off blows from the willow switch, from the flailing fists. If she cries, the blows come at her harder and stronger and the voice yells, "Quit your bawling or I will give you something to really cry about."

If she holds back the tears and doesn't let out a sound the blows still come and come and seem to never stop as the voice yells, "Damn it, I will show you who's boss."

When she pleads for mercy and cries out "Sorry! I'm sorry! Please, I'm sorry, sorry, sorry," the voice yells, "You think you are sorry? You don't even know what the word means! I'll teach you sorry." She is dragged from the corner then, and she leaves, not physically, but she still leaves.

The image fades and I look down at the child. I stroke her hair, take the shawl from the corner of the couch, cover her and pull the blanket close around her. I look at her; I see how peaceful and beautiful she looks in her sleep.

"Sorry," I say under my breath. "I see your goodness and I don't want you to ever lose it. I really don't believe in meanness but it lives deeply in my bones and I am mean. I am so sorry."

I slip off the couch, look down at her, tears streaming down my face. I go to the bedroom and pull down an old suitcase from the closet shelf. I put it on the bed with the lid open and throw some clothes in. After I snap it shut I go to the bathroom and find a small cosmetic bag. I fill it with a toothbrush, some toothpaste and miscellaneous pills, a bottle of lotion and my red lipstick. I collect it all together: the suitcase, the cosmetic bag, my purse, and I walk to the couch.

I bend down and kiss the sleeping child. I whisper to her, "I don't believe in meanness and I am mean." I walk to the door and take one last look at her and leave. I don't lock the door, I just leave. I get into the car, press the starter, back out of the driveway onto the dark street, and I start driving. I drive for about an hour.

In my head there is a constant refrain between that child of long ago and the words "I don't believe in meanness and I am mean." The image of the sleeping child comes and goes. I stop at a filling station and go to the phone booth.

I pick up the receiver and dial 911. "I want to report an abandoned child at 7956 Rollingwood Drive in San Pablo, California. No, I don't have any information; no, I don't know who she is. Just send someone for her. Goodbye." I hang up the phone. I return to the car and I head south.

Modern Creation Myth

Lilith sat on the beach in the warm southern sun. She occasionally lifted herself from the sand, moved to the brilliant blue-green water and sat in the shallow waves as they lapped her buttocks, her thighs, and curled around her toes. As she looked around, she felt an uneasy satisfaction in this new world, the planet she and God had agreed to call Earth.

Her mind went to thoughts of God. "What a strange name," she thought. Both of them had chosen their own names. God had wanted to choose hers: "Goddess!" No thank you! That was when the struggle began. She was not going to be an appendage of anyone no matter how divinely created they might be. After all, she, too, was a Divine Creation.

Determinedly, she was going to have her own name. She loved the musical sound of Lilith. Sometimes her name was like tinkling bells, yet other times like an echoing battle cry. God was not an interesting name at all and no way was he going to lay "Goddess" on her.

Her mind turned to the creation process. It had been trial and error. Why the Divine wanted her and God to do this enormous project together was totally beyond her understanding. In spite of warnings not to question divine wisdom, Lilith was not one to accept anything easily. It had been nothing but challenge, disagreement, and compromise from start to finish.

God was so difficult, spoiled and peevish when he didn't get his own way. The heavens filled with their conflict. Their roaring became thunder; the sparks that flew were soon lightning flashing across the heavens. Sometimes there would be a great groan from the Divine. Finally, it was done ... or sort of done ... .

Lilith caught herself thinking of improvements she might just sneak behind God's back or subtle ways she might add a little excitement, a little spice to the whole project. Whenever she made a suggestion to God, it was met with stern disapproval. There were hundreds of major mistakes, and millions of little mistakes. Lilith was most uneasy about the little mistakes. They seemed so unpredictable. The big mistakes were so glaring that it would not take evolution long to handle them. The little ones might go for millions of years before anyone even recognized they were mistakes, and by then it could be too late.

Finally, in exhaustion, she came to the shore to rest. She hoped Eve would be able to manage both God and Adam. She felt some concern, but not enough to keep her from a long nap.

Adam was weary. This woman Eve was a handful. God had quietly told him to call her "Woman." Lilith had suggested she choose her own name. Eve was exploring all possibilities. She thought of Lillian, after Lilith. She just didn't want to be named after anyone. She reflected, selected, discarded, and reviewed her ideas and still she could not find a name that totally suited her. She knew she would not settle for "Woman."

God was enjoying this new planet. He was quite pleased with himself. Of course, if he had not had to contend with Lilith, it would be even more extraordinary. How could anyone be so opinionated, so stubborn, have such a thick skull? God was sure he was the superior one and knew the exact wishes of the Divine. Lilith had been a real trial for him. He did not question Divine Wisdom but this time he did not understand it even remotely.

When Adam appeared looking angry, confused, and frustrated, God understood immediately. Of course Adam was right. It was Eve that was causing such grief.

"God, isn't there any way you can help me with Eve? I am worn out. Nothing works. No matter what I do she has an opinion on it and is so stubborn. I don't understand why you created such a difficult creature for me. I need help."

God studied Adam, who at that moment looked so small, insignificant, and lonely. God was quiet for a long time and finally spoke. "Lilith is off gallivanting around and probably won't be back for a while. When you rest this night give Eve a drink that I will prepare for you. While she sleeps soundly, I will change her so she's more manageable. When she awakes she will be a different person."

Eve wasn't very sleepy. She couldn't understand Adam. He was yawning, suggesting an earlier than usual bedtime. At first she just ignored him, and then he became laughable in his efforts to get her to go to bed. She began to roll on the grass with delight and laughter. As usual, Adam spoiled her fun by sulking. She apologized, tongue in cheek. "How did I get stuck with this creature?" she wondered, "He is so humorless, no fun at all." She was sleepy after all the activity, and was pleasantly surprised when Adam offered her a drink. Usually it was, "Hey Eve, bring me a drink, will you?"

It was a long night. Eve slept soundly while Adam watched her with excitement. Finally, he dreamed of the new woman he hoped would be lying beside him in the morning. When morning came, Eve opened her eyes and looked around, feeling different but not knowing exactly how. She impulsively leaned over and kissed Adam. Adam opened his eyes in amazement. Eve was smiling down on him with adoration in her eyes. Tentatively Adam looked at her and wondered if it had really worked. God did not see any reason to tell Adam that it was not quite perfect.

Adam tentatively referred to Eve as "my Woman." She smiled and did not protest. Inside, Adam was thrilled. He now had the woman he wanted. He tested this reality often by ordering Eve around, getting her to wait on him, prepare food for him, and in general, be available to his every need. When he called Lilith "Goddess" Eve did not protest. Adam kept his promise to God. Eve accepted both the label "Woman" and began to refer to Lilith as "Goddess." Both God and Adam were smug.

Life in Paradise became lazy, placid, satisfying, and perhaps a little boring. God slept a lot and got fatter and more and more indolent. If Adam thought, "I wish Eve was more amorous," she became more amorous. If Eve wished for new or more interesting fruits or berries, the new berry or piece of fruit would appear. God observed his creation with smug satisfaction. Lilith was nowhere around. It was peaceful and there was no conflict. He grudgingly admitted he missed Lilith. He dismissed this unwelcome thought and lay down to take another long nap. In his mind it was now his creation. Lilith was in no hurry to reunite with God either, even though in a strange and puzzling way, she missed him, too.

Eve became more and more discontent. She could not name the problem. She felt restless, agitated and carried an unexpressed irritation at both Adam and God. She did not understand what was happening. After all, wasn't everything perfect? She wandered aimlessly around Eden looking for something, not quite certain what. Even Adam was getting more and more listless.

Lilith finally returned. When she saw God asleep snoring loudly, even fatter than she remembered, she wondered to herself, "How could I have missed him?" There was an edge of disgust in her thoughts.

Now that she was back in Eden, she began to fume. Eve was not the being she had left behind. Lilith stormed, creating a tornado in her fury. The tornado rapidly turned into an ice storm and woke everyone. Lilith, stomping up to God, demanded, "What happened here?" God stretched leisurely, smiled and said with feigned innocence, "I don't know what you are talking about."

Lilith glared at him for a long moment. He glared back. Lilith decided the direct approach was not going to work. She thundered away to think, plot, and scheme.

Eve continued her aimless wandering. Adam began to miss the old Eve. "At least she offered a little spice to life. She was stubborn, that was true," Adam reflected, "but she was more interesting, more fun, and pushed me to be more of myself." Now he just felt bored, slightly depressed and had little or no energy. He watched God and thought, "We are just getting to be a couple of fat old farts." Adam did not enjoy these scary thoughts.

Eve sat under a tree looking up at the forbidden fruit on the tree in the center of Eden. The fruit looked more and more delicious. Her mouth watered and as she gazed at the fruit, her longing grew. It did not take much for the beautiful snake to convince her that the fruit was forbidden because God was afraid that someone might be smarter than he. At that moment Adam appeared, complaining, and whining. Inside, Eve felt a place of rebellion stirring. The snake kept coaxing her to go ahead and eat the delicious-looking fruit. Whispering and hissing, the snake encouraged Eve to insist that Adam eat the fruit with her.

Eve began to feel a little of her old self. She knew better than to demand or argue. She knew the way to Adam's heart and compliance was through seduction and the promise of sex. She smiled at him, stroked his chest, pinched his buttocks and other places she knew might arouse him. She softly blew on his neck and in his ear. She caressed him and fondled him, smiling and teasing. Then as abruptly as she had started, she stopped, pouting, "I want some of the fruit first."

Adam began protesting, "It would upset God and then what would happen?"

Eve persisted. Adam protested. Finally, Adam agreed. After all, what could God possible do? Maybe scold them, yell at them, kick them out of the Garden? At that moment Adam thought, "Good! I am pretty bored anyway." Adam was surprised. He did not know this thought lived inside him. He took Eve by the waist and they walked to the tree and ate the fruit. Lilith shed the skin of the beautiful snake and God woke up from one of his endless naps knowing it was all over.

Touching the World ...

... thought pieces

Abortion:
A Legal—and Moral—Decision

I have been following the struggle over whether or not abortion should be legal. What are the moral and legal issues? It seems the rationale for not legalizing abortion or for challenging Roe v. Wade and many laws, both at the federal and the state levels, is to protect life. I assume it is believed that this would give government the right to establish jurisdiction over a woman's decisions not only regarding her body, but also over decisions regarding what is in the best interest of herself and the life she is carrying in her body, regardless of her marital status.

The choice and decisions government wants to control and legislate may impact the quality of life for the woman, the child she is carrying and, if she is married, the well-being of her family. This would not have a short-term impact; these decisions could change her life or the well-being of her family for many years.

It seems if the law insists a woman gives birth to an unwanted child, or if she abandons her child, or if she has limited resources, the child will not be able to thrive and will suffer significantly as a result of the decision made by representatives of the government. With the laws that prohibit abortion and a woman's choice in regards to her own life, the birth and life of a child will create unnecessary suffering for everyone involved. The law prohibiting abortion then becomes an act of cruelty without regard for what is in the best interest of everyone involved, including the unborn child.

When a child is born into a situation of limited resources and its basic needs, as well as the right to thrive, are not honored, then it becomes the responsibility of the state. The legislators who support laws against abortion, and take away a woman's right to decide whether it was in the best interest for her and for the unborn child must now provide these new beings with the quality of life that will support their well-being and thriving—not just existing, but thriving.

The state has a responsibility to make sure the mother and her family, if she has one, have the necessary resources to provide a quality of life matching the same standards as state officials and leaders have determined is adequate for their own families. This would include a comfortable single-family home in a middle class neighborhood, adequate nurturing, classes for parents to improve their parenting skills, comprehensive health care, and an environment where the child can thrive physically, emotionally and intellectually. This should be the goal: the child has the same benefits as children born to a legislator or a governor, so that her child has the necessary support to become an active contributing member of society.

Everyone in the family must benefit from the laws legislators pass regarding abortion. The benefits needed to care for the child and its single low-income parent must provide the resources necessary for her to be home with the child for the first two years of life and she must be eligible for job training or college opportunities. Included in the benefits would be the same benefits as those provided to a child born into a family with the means to support it. If laws are passed that do not allow abortions, then the government must assume responsibility and provide for those affected by the law.

It must be remembered that if a woman agrees to a sexual relationship, it does not mean she has agreed to pregnancy. The pregnancy involves both a man and a woman. Neither can assume the other has taken responsibility for birth control. If a pregnancy occurs, the man must be required to contribute to the well-being of the baby to the best of his ability. If he has limited resources, the state must make up the difference and make sure the unwelcome child has the same benefits and resources as the children of state officials.

An important factor for a child is contact with both biological parents. If the relationship between the two parties is friendly and respectful, then they will be able to establish how both of them will be involved in the child's life. The state must provide the resources to support both parents, enabling both of them to participate in the child's growth and development. When the participants are not friendly, or in the case of date rape or any other kind of sexual violence, it is in the best interest of the child, all parties involved, and society, for the couple to be provided the resources to help them work through the anger, pain and deep hurt that may have resulted and would likely have a negative affect on the child born of this union.

Under no circumstance may either party be denied support or available resources. Anti-abortion laws of the state are responsible for creating the situations that are not in the best interest of those involved.

If everything I mention in writing about the cruelty and disregard for life created by anti-abortion legislators and governors for the well-being of a newborn is resolved, then I might consider supporting abortion being illegal. Currently not having legalized abortion becomes an opportunity for children to suffer, for families to suffer, and for women to be pushed into making cruel and inhumane decisions.

I cannot in good conscience support the right-to-life movement until it supports that every child born under *any* conditions has the right to thrive. Being deprived of that right is cruel, inhumane and unethical behavior on the part of those who have created and perpetuated the situation by not legalizing abortion and not supporting other laws and conditions that benefit all children and their parents.

Colin Kaepernick

Verses from Langston Hughes' poem:

Let America Be America Again

Let America be America again—
O, let America be America again—
The land that has never been yet—
And yet must be—the land where every man is free.
The land that's mine—the poor man's, Indian's, Negro's, ME—
Who made America.
Whose sweat and blood, whose faith and pain,
Whose hand in the foundry, whose plow in the rain,
Must bring back our mighty dream again.
Sure, call me any ugly name you choose—
The steel of freedom does not stain.
From those who live like leeches on the people's lives,
We must take back our land again,
America!
Oh, yes,
I say it plain,
America never was America to me,
And yet I swear this oath—
America will be!

1619-20	Slaves in Virginia. Africans brought to Jamestown are first in Britain's North American colonies.
January 1, 1863	Emancipation proclamation to free slaves.
1964	Civil Rights Act
2016–18	"Black Lives Matter" movement
September, 2016	Colin Kaepernick knelt on one knee rather than stand and salute the flag.

Many years ago I heard Noam Chomsky, a professor at MIT whom I particularly admired, respond to those who wanted him to censor publicly a book written to prove that Jews were less than the "pure" White race, specifically Christians. Professor Chomsky, a Jew, replied, "I don't agree with the book, but I support the author's right to write it."

When I get angry at the dialogue, the name calling, the demonizing of others, I remember this statement and can acknowledge, sometimes not with much ease, the importance of the right to speak and not be censored. There can be no democracy without freedom of speech. Now students are standing on the steps of universities in this country using the Nazi salute and carrying signs against Jews. This is their right. I may not approve of it, or like it, but it is their right. Punishment is not the answer, but education is—not lectures or text books, but direct experiences with those who are different from us, or whom we have demonized—open dialog and deep listening. Sharing the depth of the experiences in life that led you to where you are now.

All those messages from the time you were born until this very minute, do they help you to be the best human being you are capable of being, or do they hinder and keep you locked into old harmful ideas that hurt others and yourself? I know many of my stories from childhood lead me down paths filled with hate, mean-spirited behavior, and other ways I really did not want to be. It took many years before I knew I could let those old ways go.

On September 1, 2016, Colin Kaepernick knelt on one knee as the flag was raised. He simply knelt; he did not salute the flag or put his hand on his heart. He was calling attention to injustices against minorities, injustices that have never been healed, and are as old as this country. He is an African American man, a professional football player.

As I reflect on his action even today, I cannot think of a more appropriate, thoughtful, humble, simple way to make a statement to call attention to the many years minorities have survived injustice and continue to suffer today. The list belies belief, it is so long—Native Americans, African Americans, Japanese Americans, Mexican Americans, Mexicans, Muslims, Jews. It appears only Caucasians have escaped. It is apparent no one escapes permanently.

Colin Kaepernick paid a high price for his simple act of calling attention to the need for justice. His was an act that easily fits the definition of free speech: no violent acting-out, no fighting, no name-calling or demonizing of anyone. And yet, I don't believe he has played football since 2017. I know other players joined him and I applaud them. It would be difficult to give up the hard-earned right to have enough money to live like white Americans, send your kids to good schools, have health care for your family, and live in safe neighborhoods.

Most, if not all, the owners of NFL teams are White, rich, and powerful, as are most NFL officials. Most of the football players are African American or some other social minority. The players are the only ones who risk devastating, crippling injuries that may cost them their careers, or risk the threat of repeated concussions that can lead to early dementia or other cognitive problems. They risk having their lives significantly shortened. Not one of the owners or officials takes those risks. They get rich off of the men who do.

Yet, for a group of men who have been marginalized, often the only jobs available had been the poorest jobs, and the hope of going to college seemed impossible and often was. Now you have a chance to make a decent living, be admired for your skill, and above all live in a way you have longed to live, a life like White Americans often live as seen on television. To have a place in society, to be paid well, to have a nice home and to be able to give your family a life you never even knew existed must feel pretty good. When conflict arises, silence seems the best choice; no one wants to rock the boat. I certainly can't blame them. I imagine many slaves felt the same way.

And yes, this reminds me of slavery. A group of White men getting rich and having total control over the well-being of a large group of minority men. This year when it came time to fire coaches, guess who made up the biggest percentage of coaches being fired: African Americans.

A few days ago I used the ride service, Lyft. The driver was an African American. I love taking alternative means of transportation. I have met refugees who are here because they helped American soldiers in the various wars that rage across the world. I have met women who left their homeland after being raped, beaten, not once or twice, but time after time, until they found a way out. I have heard about their children and the families they had to leave behind. I have talked to students, men holding down two jobs, and the various ways many people patch together enough to make a life work.

Well, I mentioned to this African American driver that minority football players ought to start their own league, earn money for themselves, and be in charge of how the game is played to keep them safe from injury. I knew it would be hard and they might have to start out playing in borrowed college and high school stadiums. I believed they would have enough support, and they would have a say! His response was, "I don't think anyone would let them." The truth of that statement hit me in my heart.

When I was teaching sixth grade in a school in one of the many Valley towns that crawl up the center of California, I became a football coach for the sixth-grade boys. All the sixth-grade teachers were women and none of them were interested in coaching football. The principal asked for a volunteer; otherwise, the boys would not have a team. I volunteered and that night read everything I could about football in the *World Book Encyclopedia*. I was amazed to find that the heart and soul of the game were not in the violence, but in the strategy, the ability to think fast and, when something was not working, to find an immediate new working strategy.

The teams played flag football and I highly recommend it as the game in high school and college, and if the truth was known, I would recommend it for professional players as well. No one got a concussion, or a broken bone. They had a good time and they loved figuring out plays, being creative thinkers, coaching each other and supporting one another. No one was ever pushed down to the ground, or had an elbow in his face, or an arm around his neck.

Our team lost the last game of the season. We came in second. On the ride back to our school, the son of the high school basketball coach was sitting in the back of the van, pounding his fist into the palm of his hand. "If only we had a man coach, we would have won," he repeated over and over again. Prejudice had been passed on to him from his father. But then, again, I was not allowed to wear slacks as I coached. I had to wear a dress or skirt and blouse. Biases and prejudice ran rampant in the early 1950s. I seriously thought of flunking that boy in PE, except I knew where he had learned what he was saying.

Needless to say, I still love football. I don't love watching a player lying on the field in obvious pain. I don't like knowing that many players never recover from the multitude of injuries they suffer. I hate knowing that some of them will suffer from early dementia, or a stroke, or some other condition or ailment connected to a brain injury. I can barely stand the idea that it is okay for players to be seriously injured as long as there is money to be made.

I believe flag football would be a much better game, requiring more skill, more creativity, more problem-solving skills. Further, I believe after the many years I have watched football and been interested in the sport that in every game I have watched, every player is capable of playing a better game with a different skill set and with less likelihood of serious injury. I would love it if a group of African Americans started their own league with less emphasis on violence and brute physical force, more emphasis on skill and strategy. I would especially like it if they did not discriminate against other races, whether their skin be white, brown, yellow, or red.

Not only do I still love football, I still believe strongly in Freedom of Speech. I don't always like how that right is used and abused. When it is used to put down others, call names, out-and-out lie, use abusive and horrible language to attack another, I do not like it. I remind myself I don't have to listen to them, patronize their businesses, socialize with them, or include them in my life in any way. What I have to do is defend their right to speak.

I think we all need to be educated about our humanness, our responsibility to each other and how to support the best of our humanity. Schools need a curriculum where the emphasis is on accepting ourselves and others, on recognizing we are living in the same house, and on the Golden Rule as being one of our guides to appropriate, loving, compassionate behavior, even to our enemies. Schools need a program that helps us understand our fears and our need at times to make others bad or wrong, and shows us a path to joint cooperative efforts for the good of all who live here or anywhere else.

Missing ...

... and forgetting

Missing and Forgetting
May 3, 2018

I will miss the sunlight through the trees.
> *the brilliance of fall, rust, red, orange and gold*
> *the bare branches against the sky.*

I will remember the wonder of watching one lone leaf fall.

I will miss the sound of the wind blowing around the house.
> *the crashing of waves against the rocks*
> *the sun setting, reflecting on the water.*

I will remember the awe of seeing the ocean for the first time.

I will miss the lush hills of spring.
> *the summer-parched hills*
> *the first snowfall.*

I will remember the serenity and quiet as the snow piled higher and higher.

I will miss the sunrise when I wake in the morning.
> *the sunset over the trees*
> *the blue of the sky and the clouds.*

I will remember driving watching the sun set on one side, the moon rise on the other.

I will miss the full moon in the fall.

    the new moon in a winter sky

    the changing moon from no moon to full moon.

I will remember a cat my family named Moonie, because the moon followed us home.

I will miss the solstice, both summer and winter.

    miss the longest day now getting shorter

    miss the shortest day now getting longer.

I will remember the seasons of life.

I will miss beautiful music.

    soaring voices and violins playing

    the soprano at operas.

I will remember the tears of hearing a beautiful song played or sung.

I will miss having coffee and the paintings on the wall.

    the vibrant colors of the paint

    the feel of a brush gliding over paper.

I will remember the thrill of color and brush.

I will miss the moment of finishing a wonderful book.

    the emotional impact of a book on my soul

    the visions created while reading.

I will remember the longing in my heart to create something, anything.

I will miss this earth and the smell of it.

    the feel and the look of this earth

    the beauty of this planet.

I hope I remember somewhere and sometime what it meant to be here.

Acknowledgments

The following is a list of all those who got this book ready for publishing and those who supported me and helped me so it was not totally impossible at age 93.

Jan Tannarome, who kept me in line, improving my mind with her listening and editing of the book. My gratitude to you.

Kit Bailey who was proofreader, editor, and great support. He did an excellent job, and was kind and thoughtful throughout the entire endeavor. I cannot sing his praises enough, or express my gratitude enough!

Julie Valin, who has helped with the publishing process. She has been generous with her skills and our working together has been a delight.

Anne Adden is the most recent member of the group. Anne's skills, design talents and creativity enhanced all the activities involved in getting the book published.

All of these people enriched my life, improved my writing and brought joy to the process.

In addition, I would like to add my children: Char Ghio, Beth Thompson, and Tony Ghio; my grandchildren Nicole and Taylor Thompson, and my great-grandchildren, Ava, Cairo and Judah Ubaka. To all of you, be loved and blessed, and have many moments of happiness.

Thanks to the Unitarian Universalist Community of the Mountains and my many friends there. All of you hold a place in my heart. May you be blessed with love and wisdom.

May Susan Suntree be blessed. She reminded me every day to write the first book and now here she is, still in my life, encouraging me, keeping me on track and inspiring me by her dedication to her own work.

www.ingramcontent.com/pod-product-compliance
Lightning Source LLC
Chambersburg PA
CBHW031334160426
43196CB00007B/689